CARPETGATE

The True Story Of Ireland's First Witness
PROTECTION PROGRAMME

By

Brendan McGoldrick

Copyright © 2025

Brendan McGoldrick

All Rights Reserved

No part of this publication may be reproduced, distributed, or transmitted in any form or by any means, including photocopying, recording, or other electronic or mechanical methods, without the prior written permission of the publisher.

DEDICATION

I would like to dedicate this book to my late mother, Breda Davis, who showed great courage and wisdom in the face of adversity and held the family together.

ACKNOWLEDGMENTS

I would like to thank Paul Williams, Ireland's leading crime writer, for his kind permission to use material from his books, which I did sparingly.

ABOUT THE AUTHOR

Brendan McGoldrick was educated at one of Ireland's most famous rugby schools, St Mary's College, Rathmines, the College of Commerce, Rathmines, and the Institute of Technology Tallaght. Despite being caught up in his major financial scandal in my mid-twenties, which put an end to his financial career, Bredan never lost his interest in finance. He has five financial qualifications, which include a first-class honours degree in finance and accounting. Brendan is now a retiree, which gave him the time and space to research and write this book.

TABLE OF CONTENTS

PREFACE..vi

CHAPTER 1 Kelly's Carpet Supermarket 1

CHAPTER 2 Kelly's Carpetdrome 7

CHAPTER 3 Kelly's Carpetdrive-In..17

CHAPTER 4 The Reckoning...36

CHAPTER 5 Haughey of Kinsealy..56

CHAPTER 6 Nolle Prosequi 80

CHAPTER 7 The Aftermath 91

PREFACE

This book is based on events that took place approximately forty years ago and presents the true story behind three high-profile High Court cases that occurred over three consecutive years: 1982, 1983, and 1984. These three cases were collectively known as *the Kelly Case*. Arising from these cases is the Irish State's first-ever witness protection programme. This witness protection programme is not recognised by the Irish State. This book explores the reasons for this and discovers one of the biggest cover-ups in the history of the Irish State.

This is a true story and is not based on fiction. This is a story worth telling, and it can be told at any time, even after forty years, as I believe it holds significant historical interest. The readers can make up their own minds, draw their own conclusions, and pass their own judgements.

A special word of thanks to the members of the *Garda Special Task Force* who put their lives at risk, on a daily basis for almost three years, for my protection.

—Brendan McGoldrick

CHAPTER 1

KELLY'S CARPET SUPERMARKET

"If you tell a lie big enough and keep repeating it, people will eventually come to believe it."
—Joseph Goebbels, Nazi propagandist

It was August 1979. I was an accounts clerk working for a transport company on Boundary Road in Dublin's East Wall. I had just turned 23 years of age, and I was living with my parents, in an apartment over their residential newsagent's shop on the North Circular Road behind *The Nurses' Home* in the Mater Hospital. It was a long journey to Dublin's East Wall, so I had been keeping my eye out for a job closer to home. I spotted an advertisement for an accounts position with *Kelly's Carpetdrome*, also located on the North Circular Road. I took pen to paper and wrote a letter, applying for the job.

The stretch of road between Dorset Street and Doyle's Corner was a hive of activity. It contained the Mater Hospital, Mountjoy Prison, Mountjoy Garda Station, a Bank of Ireland branch, an Allied Irish Bank branch, a shopping centre, and Kelly's Carpetdrome, which was the largest private sector employer in the area.

Paddy Creagh, a Carpetdrome employee, contacted me to organise an interview. An interview was arranged for a couple of days later. Paddy Creagh started the interview and was later joined by Matt Kelly, who appeared to be the proprietor of the business. Paddy Delaney, a chartered accountant, also joined the interview. After some deliberations, I was offered the job, and the terms were agreed upon. I started work at the end of August. The vacancy had arisen over the resignation of my predecessor, Eileen Hogg, who had left the firm to immigrate to Canada.

Kelly's Carpetrome was a medium-sized department store on Dublin's northside. It consisted of three departments: carpets, furniture, and soft furnishings. Its outstanding feature was its indoor car park, which was a huge attraction to customers in an area short of car parking spaces. Although the store had the appearance of a large warehouse, it had retail frontage onto the North Circular Road through three shop fronts. The carpets were housed on the first floor and the furniture on the ground floor of the main body of the premises, which was flanked by the back of Dalymount Park on the left and by Phibsborough shopping centre on the right. Overall, it was a considerable undertaking. The premises originally were a depot for the old Dublin tram company.

The Kelly family consisted of five brothers, Desmond, Matthew, Eamon, Gerald, and Thomas, along with three sisters, Patsy, Gretta, and Joan. Matthew Kelly, Eamon Kelly, and their brother-in-law, Paul Jackson, who was married to their sister, Joan, were involved in the Carpetdrome.

Matthew Kelly, although neither a shareholder nor a director, was the driving force behind the business. He was tall, well-built, and possessed good looks. He had charismatic leadership traits and resembled the film star Steve McQueen very closely. Matthew Kelly had tremendous business acumen and was also an excellent carpet buyer. Therefore, all major business decisions were made by him. He was also an excellent property speculator and developer. He had an excellent grasp of current and business affairs and could easily hold his own with the captains of Irish industry. The warehouse, car park, and retail units were owned by Monck properties, which Matt Kelly controlled. The Carpetdrome had two directors, Eamon Kelly and Paul Jackson. Matt Kelly was not a director of Carpetdrome, but signed most of the company's cheques; the other signatory was his brother, Eamon Kelly. Matt Kelly was the buyer and de facto managing director and was known to the general public as the *Carpet King*.

The Carpetdrome commenced trading in October 1976. This followed a previous Kelly family venture into the carpet trade called *Kelly's Carpet Supermarket,* which began trading in a car sales retail unit on the opposite side of the North Circular Road, facing the entrance to St Peter's Church in December 1973. This enterprise ceased trading in 1976 and went into liquidation in 1977, with a claim of IR£200,000 for VAT against the Revenue Commissioners. Fergal Gaynor, a chartered accountant, was appointed liquidator, and he disputed the Revenue Commissioners' VAT claim in its entirety. The VAT claim has never been finally determined, although the Revenue Commissioners had at all times the means and power to press their claim to a conclusion had they elected to do so.

Desmond Kelly was also involved in Kelly's Carpet Supermarket. Following the cessation of Kelly's Carpet Supermarket business, there was a split in the Kelly family. Matt Kelly set up the Carpetdrome at Doyle's Corner, and Desmond Kelly set up his own carpet business in premises at Cross Guns Bridge, not too far away. The two remaining brothers, Gerald Kelly and Tomas Kelly, had totally different careers—Gerald worked as an employee for Des Kelly in the Cross Guns bridge store, and Tomas worked for the Irish Press.

So, the Carpetdrome was trading for almost three years when I joined in 1979. The firm was a hive of activity, with fifty people earning a living, either directly or indirectly, such as carpet-fitting sub-contractors. The Carpetdrome operated a fleet of six vans, with a fitter and helper assigned to each, and this was supplemented by as many as six independent subcontracting fitters. Containers, full of rolls of carpet, arrived on a daily basis and were promptly unloaded by one of the forklifts. The rolls were then left on the floor of the car park. These rolls were then moved up onto the first floor when a rack became available to house them.

Carpetdrome was advertised each weekend in the national newspapers, with the Evening Press being the favourite paper. This drew huge crowds, particularly on a Sunday. The Carpetdrome had an advantage over its competitors, as other department stores did not open on Sundays; therefore, there were rich pickings for salesmen, most of which went to the local hostelries and bookmakers.

I later established from the late, and very popular, manufacturers' agent, Richard Byrne, that Stoddard carpets, a UK manufacturer, had done some market research and had come to the conclusion that Carpetdrome was the largest retailer of carpets in Western Europe. This was some achievement in a short period of time. I took up my duties at the end of August 1979 in a position that today would be described as an Accounts Payable role.

I had spent three and a half years at the College of Commerce Rathmines, where I did business studies, so there was a little more expected of me than being an accounts clerk. I found an accounts system that was very basic. Supplier's invoices, which were paid, were put in a bundle along with the supplier statement, and with a remittance advice listing the invoices paid, the cheque amount, and the cheque number, and these were all clipped together and placed in a twin-lock file in a filing cabinet.

The objective of the accounting system was to ensure that no invoice was paid twice, and the system in operation served no other purpose. Purchase invoices were recorded in a daybook for VAT purposes. Bank lodgements were recorded in another daybook, also for VAT purposes. A cash receipts basis was used for calculating VAT. VAT returns had not been made for several months. Wage records were okay, but again, returns were in arrears. There was no creditors' ledger, which would show amounts owing to each supplier and the total amount owing to all suppliers. There was no nominal ledger nor any stock-taking records, which meant that the Carpetdrome never had final accounts, such as a profit and loss account and a balance sheet, even after three years of trading.

Faced with these circumstances, I decided to acquire a Kalamazoo bookkeeping system and to attempt to build up an accounting system by rewriting the records from scratch, which obviously meant going back three years. With the benefit of hindsight, I believe that this was a poor decision, as events unfolded at a rapid pace in 1980.

Carpetdrome did not own the premises from which it traded, nor did it pay any rent to the landlord, Monck Properties, which owned the premises. Matthew Kelly was the major shareholder in Monck Properties. Carpetdrome had only two issued shares and an overdraft facility of £100,000 with the AIB branch in Phibsborough. I later found out that this overdraft was covered by a deposit of £100,000 in the AIB branch, which meant it wasn't really a proper overdraft facility. The only other sources of finances were the six leases on the Carpetdrome fleet of vans. For such a large undertaking, Carpetdrome had no capital structure.

A second office was located on the carpet sales floor. This was the office where the business was controlled from. Orders were dispatched from here, and a receptionist handled incoming telephone calls. Balances collected by carpet fitters were handed in to this office, and it was a hive of activity. In effect, this was the place where the real accounting took place.

CHAPTER 2

KELLY'S CARPETDROME

"In deepest, darkest Africa, where Jesus Christ is still unknown, Kelly's Carpetdrome is a household name."
—Matt Kelly, 1980

In February 1980, I was sent to the UK to work for a carpet wholesaler called *Roundwood Carpets Limited* in Ossett, Yorkshire. Yorkshire was the centre of carpet manufacturing in the United Kingdom. Brian Smith was the managing director of Roundwood Carpets. He was a former sales representative for Wilkinson Warburton Carpets. Roundwood Carpets was a carpet wholesaler, selling carpets to small carpet shops in the Yorkshire area. It traded from a warehouse owned by a company called *Gladsigns Ltd*. Gladsigns, in turn, was owned by Matt Kelly. Similar to the arrangement between Carpetdrome and Monck Properties, Roundwood Carpets was a tenant of Gladsigns, but paid no rent. In return for this concession, Roundwood sold carpets to Carpetdrome at cost, plus a small markup and the freight charge. About one-third of Roundwood's sales were to Dublin.

The directors of Roundwood Carpets were Brian Smith and his wife, Paula. However, Matt Kelly regarded Roundwood Carpets as his own business. Therefore, I was ordered to Roundwood Carpets to have a look at the books, notwithstanding the fact that I had no legal authority to do so. On arrival, Brian Smith picked me up at Leeds-Bradford airport, having been advised only that morning that I was coming. This caused consternation in Roundwood as the books were in their accountant's office for the purpose of an audit. When they were collected from the accountant's office, I commenced a reconciliation between the Carpetdrome records and their corresponding account in Roundwood's books.

I spent two weeks in England working on this. What I discovered astonished me: about half the money paid to Roundwood did not come from the Carpetdrome bank account, but from other sources. I estimate this amount to be in the region of IR£500,000. Roundwood's annual trade with Dublin was around IR£1m. Roundwood's accountant, Frank Dobby, was concerned about this and was thinking of calling in the English police. I persuaded him not to do so when I agreed to reflect the unaccounted money as unrecorded sales in Carpetdrome books. He wanted signed undertakings from Carpetdrome directors to give effect to this, and in due course, these were provided. Later, I was to discover that a similar amount, IR£500,000, was paid to the UK's largest wholesaler, Mercado, and this amount also did not appear in Carpetdrome's books.

Roundwood also served another very important purpose. Navan carpets, under pressure from Irish retailers, refused to supply Carpetdrome. Roundwood ordered carpet rolls from Navan, who shipped them to Roundwood, who in turn shipped them back to Carpetdrome. This was a feasible operation as there was a price cartel in operation, involving departmental stores, in Ireland, which overpriced expensive Axminster carpets.

The Roundwood operation helped break this cartel and, thus, reduce prices for ordinary punters. Navan carpets discreetly sent in staff into the Carpetdrome, and they got the product numbers off the rolls. When they established that the carpets had gone through Roundwood, they halted the supplies. Roundwood had huge orders placed with Navan for several months in advance, totalling at least IR£1m. These orders were not fulfilled. Navan also refused to pay the local agents' commission on the cancelled orders. The English agent took Navan Carpets to court and won his case. Navan had to pay the agent IR£50,000 in commission and pay the costs of the action. Purchasing carpets from Roundwood and other UK suppliers had another major advantage: there was no VAT at source when the VAT rate was 25%.

I stayed in a local bed and breakfast near Ossett, which was fine, but trips to Leeds were awkward due to the Yorkshire Ripper being at large, who gripped the city in fear, leaving bars, restaurants, and nightclubs empty. The best advice was not to approach women unless introduced. I hadn't seen anything like this in forty years until the current lockdown restrictions were introduced. The other great talking point was the miners' strike. Opinion was divided, with some on the miners' side and others who felt that their huge wages were unsustainable. Brian Smith's carpet warehouse held David Harvey's furniture after he broke up with his wife. He was the current Leeds United goalkeeper, having taken over from Gary Sprake.

I got the chance to visit Elland Road for a first division match between Leeds United and Brighton. Brian also introduced me to former Leeds United striker David McNiven, and the Scotsman lambasted me over the Provisional IRA campaign in Northern Ireland, which had nothing to do with me.

One dark February evening, Brian Smith and I went for a walk in a Leeds suburb. He pointed at a house in the distance that was heavily floodlit. I thought the floodlighting was for tennis courts. Brian then explained to me that it was the home of the former Northern Ireland secretary, Roy Mason, who was under round-the-clock protection. It was certainly a taste of things to come.

I returned to Dublin, having discovered the discrepancy between Carpetdrome and Roundwood accounts. I found that a second set of sales receipt books was kept in my office. These books had the prefix '0' on the invoice number to differentiate them from the legitimate sales books, which had the prefix '1'. The sales books with the prefix 0 were referred to by staff as the *'hooky books'* or *'Eamon's Books.'* So not only were there two sets of books, but there was a second accounting system in operation. This second accounting system was managed from the main office on the sales floor. In this office, Eamon Kelly presided over the whole operation like an operations manager, but there was a difference: he managed with an iron fist. A salesman, Derek Reddin, who made a costly error, was punished with a pellet in his rear end fired from a gun. A carpet fitter, Albert Harcourt, who made another costly mistake, was thrown into a tank full of freezing water, in the middle of winter, as punishment. So, an atmosphere of fear stalked the firm, and Eamon Kelly was affectionately referred to by the staff as '*Bullet Head.*'

It was about this time that one of the salesmen tipped me off that the Carpetdrome was a front for organised crime. Locals in the bars around Phibsborough told me that the Gardaí said that the Carpetdrome was funded from bank robberies, and I certainly would not dispute that. I kept my distance from the sales office and visited only once a day to get Eamon to sign cheques.

Matt Kelly was born in 1944, and Eamon Kelly in 1947. Both were brought up in Rutland Street in Summerhill in Dublin's north inner city. Both were in trouble with the law from their teens. Eamon Kelly, in his teens, was a minor but nasty criminal according to the Gardaí. By the end of his teens, he had four convictions for house and shop breaking and also for violent affray. The convictions stopped as he exited his teens, indicating that he had learned from an early age not to get caught.

Brother Matt had a similar background during his teenage years. Matt had acquired several convictions for burglary and assault in his teens. However, like his younger brother, he learned how not to get caught. Even though neither brother had convictions beyond these incidents in their youth, they were still classified as major criminals by the Gardaí. Matt boasted to me on several occasions that the criminal mind was far superior to the average mind. This suggested to me that he and his brother had been mentored by an older and more experienced criminal. I suspect that the mentor was Michael Deighan.

Eamon Kelly joined the IRA in the 1960s. When the IRA and its political wing, Sinn Féin, split into two factions, the Provisional IRA and the Official IRA, Eamon Kelly remained with the Official IRA. By the early 1980s, the brothers had opened carpet and furniture shops in Mary Street and Talbot Street. These shops reinforced their presence in the inner north city, where they ran an extensive protection racket. Every week, local business owners called in to these shops to make their protection payments. The Garda conducted a major investigation into this racket. However, the guards could not get any of the legitimate business owners to make a complaint against the Kelly brothers, for such was their fearsome reputation. The best the guards could get from local businesses was a private acknowledgement that they were making payments to the Kelly brothers.

The Official IRA had a secret unit called Group B[1]. The Group B unit's activities focused on providing intelligence and logistical support for criminal networks, particularly the group headed by Eamon and Matt Kelly. The Kelly gang specialised in armed robberies of cash and drink deliveries, but was willing to turn its hand to most criminal enterprises, including the burning of properties for insurance claims and

---

[1] The Lost Revolution, Brian Hanley and Scott Millar, 2010, Penguin Ireland.

counterfeiting. By the early 1980s, the Kelly gang was ranked by Gardaí as the third most serious criminal gang behind the Dunne and Cahill families.

So, I tried to plan my exit by applying for another job. I got an interview for a position with Guinness. I remember being interviewed by a Mr Ardill and a Mr McArdle, but the application was unsuccessful. Other applications did not yield an interview. Such was the reputation of Carpetrome that it made changing jobs almost impossible. It was as if one had been an inmate in the Auschwitz concentration camp, and a number had been tattooed on one's wrist. Both the stigma and the tattoo remained with you for the rest of your life. The result of all this was that I was boxed in.

Summer arrived, and Brian Smith got me two tickets for the 1980 FA Cup final between West Ham United and Arsenal, which I attended with a friend. The final was played on Saturday, 10th May 1980. This event provided a welcome respite from the office. However, things were beginning to change when I returned. Carpetdrome was struggling to pay its suppliers. Thirty-day bills were paid after sixty days, sixty-day bills were paid after ninety days, and so on. The money lodged to Carpetdrome's AIB current account was insufficient for me to pay the company's creditors. Sales representatives were calling more frequently, and relations were getting very frosty. VAT and PAYE returns were made, but there was no money to pay them. Carpetdrome was getting more and more indebted to the Revenue Commissioners. Around this time, Matt Kelly told me to get ready for a liquidation.

In June 1980, Fergal Gaynor arrived and introduced me to one of his staff, Tom Cullen. I had previously met Fergal Gaynor in his offices in Fitzwilliam Square. He said that Tom Cullen would be working on the accounts two days of the week. I showed Fergal Gaynor a statement of affairs showing liabilities of IR£650,000 and a deficit of IR£100,000. I told him that I had great doubts about the solvency of the Carpetdrome, and he pushed the document aside.

Later, on the sales floor, I told Mr Gaynor that if he was doing accounts of Carpetdrome, he would have to take into account the accounts of Roundwood Carpets because of the relationship between the two companies. There was money in the accounts of Roundwood that belonged to Matthew Kelly, and the directors of Carpetdrome had given an undertaking to bring this money into the Carpetdrome accounts. I told Mr Gaynor that he should go to Leeds and have a discussion with Mr Dobby, Roundwood's accountant. He said that he did not want to know about Roundwood and would not be concerned with Roundwood in his work. I also told Mr Gaynor that there was a bit of a fiddle going on. Mr Gaynor told me, "Never discuss the affairs of Carpetdrome with anybody." However, in High Court proceedings in 1984, Mr Gaynor denied that these conversations ever took place.

Gaynor & Tuffy Accountants were not acting as the company's auditors. Instead, they were acting as tax agents for Matthew Kelly. Tom Cullen's assignment was to prepare figures from Carpetdrome's books to be used in submissions to the Revenue Commissioners in connection with Matthew Kelly's tax affairs. Mr Cullen became aware of the difficulties the Carpetrome was having in paying its suppliers by his mere presence in the office, with suppliers' representatives calling frequently, looking for payment, and getting no satisfaction. Mr Cullen uncovered vast amounts of unpaid suppliers' cheques, totalling IR£430,000, that had bounced out of payments of IR£3,000,000. Very large sums of money were posted to a suspense account. Mr Cullen asked me why Carpetdrome had such difficulty in paying its creditors. I did not give him an answer, as his principal, Mr Gaynor, had told me previously, as discussed above, not to discuss the affairs with Carpetdrome with anybody. As well as that, it would have been suicidal to reveal the other set of books, which were under the control of Eamon Kelly in the other office on the sales floor.

Mr Cullen continued with his assignment of preparing figures for Matthew Kelly's tax case. I understood that a hearing was scheduled with the Appeal Commissioners for November 1981. Shortly before the hearing, Mr Cullen's car was broken into, and his working papers, dealing with Matthew Kelly's tax case, were stolen. This event was used to seek an adjournment from the Appeal Commissioners. A couple of weeks later, Mr Cullen finished his work and withdrew from the assignment. A year later, I was shown draft accounts for four years for the Carpetdrome from 01/11/1976 to 31/10/1980 for the first time. In December, the city sheriff was calling at the Carpetdrome with certificates issued by the Revenue Commissioners for outstanding VAT bills. After Christmas, these certificates amounted to over IR£100,000. Payments on account were made, but the Revenue applied more pressure when the sheriff arrived with a container ready to seize carpets. He failed in his mission, as any remaining rolls in the car park had been moved to the carpet department on the first floor, and the forklift with the boon was hidden. Under these circumstances, it was impossible to carry on business, and something needed to be done, so something was done.

CHAPTER 3

KELLY'S CARPETDRIVE-IN

"Hell is the truth seen too late."
—Thomas Hobbes, English Philosopher, 19th Century

The affairs of Carpetdrome were becoming increasingly difficult to manage. The sheriff had certificates for outstanding VAT for IR£100,000. The sheriff had been withdrawn after a moratorium had been agreed with the Revenue to pay the bill in six instalments of IR£17,000 over six weeks. At or about this time, Matt Kelly finished his involvement with the Carpetdrome. His brothers, Eamon and Thomas, and his brother-in-law, Paul Jackson, would continue on the carpet business. Matt Kelly would concentrate on his property business. It was proposed to give a lease on the North Circular Road premises for IR£3,000 per week. I paid a visit to the Companies Office and found a dormant company called *Kelly's Carpetdrive-In Ltd*. This company was formed on 17th February 1977. The solicitors who formed Kelly's Carpetdrive-In Ltd were W & E Bradshaw of Merrion Square, Dublin 1. I also discovered that they were the same firm of solicitors who had previously formed Kelly's Carpetdrome Ltd. Matt Kelly then got solicitor Carl O'Daly to draw up a lease between Monck Properties Ltd and Carpetdrive-In for two years and nine months, at a rent of IR£3,000 per week. The directors of Carpetdrive-In were Eamon Kelly, Paul Jackson, and Thomas Kelly.

I understood that Monck Properties would use this income to raise loans to settle outstanding taxes, and that Carpetdrive-In would be run properly, and that there would be an end to the practices in Carpetdrome that gave rise to the issues with the Revenue Commissioners. The Kelly family was very anxious for me to continue with Carpetdrive-In, and there was a promise made that I would be looked after.

Carpetdrome had spent IR£250,000 on advertising over four years. This meant that it had established Kelly Carpets as a well-known brand. As at 28/02/1981, Carpetdrome was insolvent with stock of about IR£500,000 and liabilities of over IR£600,000. I proposed to transfer the Carpetdrome stock to Carpetdrive-In, and that Carpetdrive-In would pay off the creditors of Carpetdrome, thus converting the deficit in Carpetdrome into Goodwill in the books of Carpetdrive-In. This was put into effect on 01/03/1981.

On 24th March 1981, I attended a meeting, which took place in Gaynor & Tuffy's offices. In attendance were Matthew Kelly, Eamon Kelly, Paul Jackson, Fergal Gaynor, and Pat Tuffy. I explained to Mr Gaynor the transfer of the assets and liabilities from Carpetdrome to Carpetdrive-In and that I had closed the Carpetdrome bank account on 3rd March 1981.

"The closing of the bank account would cause difficulties," Mr Gaynor said. Mr Gaynor told me to prepare analysis sheets to differentiate the sales of Carpetdrome stock by Carpetdrive-In from the sales of Carpetdrive-In's own stock, and then to reduce the sales of Carpetdrome stock to cost.

The Carpetdrome stock sold by Carpetdrive-In was then invoiced by Carpetdrome to Carpetdrive-In at cost plus 25% VAT. The payments made by Carpetdrive-In to Carpetdrome trade creditors were offset against these invoices. I became unhappy about this, and Matthew Kelly told me to stay quiet and follow Mr Gaynor's instructions. Mr Gaynor later denied that these conversations had taken place in the 1984 High Court proceedings.

The outcome of this meeting resulted in four weekly trips to Gaynor & Tuffy's offices, where Mr Gaynor reviewed the work I had done in relation to the transfer of the Carpetdrome business into Carpetdrive-In. In order to attend these meetings, I needed a lift from Siobhan O'Grady, a member of staff, in her car because of the weight and volume of books that I had to bring over, and I could not have managed them on my own. She parked her car in Fitzwilliam Square while I attended the meeting. In his evidence, in the 1984 High Court proceedings, Mr Gaynor denied that these meetings ever took place. Also, the judge dismissed these meetings, in his judgement, because I did not have accurate dates.

On 7th May 1981, Mr Gaynor arrived at around 1.30 pm at North Circular Road. We were closing down at that time due to the Bobby Sands funeral. He said that the Revenue was on the warpath. They had got wind of the transfer between Carpetdrome and Carpetdrive-In, and it had better be completed fast. A final stock-taking took place in mid-May, and most of the remaining stock was transferred around 17th May 1981. Mr Gaynor again denied that this meeting took place in the 1984 High Court proceedings.

Following the dissolution of the Dáil on 21/05/1981, Matt Kelly attended a political clinic in the Royal Oak Bar in Finglas. There, he met the outgoing Taoiseach Charles Haughey. The outcome of the meeting was that Kelly made a payment to Haughey. In return for this payment, Haughey would use his influence to have the tax bill of Carpetdrome settled at an amount much lower than what the Revenue was demanding. Matt Kelly told me this as he knew I was under pressure from the sheriff, the taxman, and the suppliers, and he could see the unfairness of all of this. What Matt Kelly did not tell me was how much he paid Mr Haughey, and I was afraid to ask him. The Stardust fire postponed the decision to hold the election in February. When the general election was eventually called in May 1981, Bobby Sands had already died on 5th May 1981. The result of this was that Mr Haughey lost the election and power. If Haughey had retained power, the Carpetdrome tax bill would have been settled quietly at a much lower amount than that which the Revenue was demanding. Garret Fitzgerald officially became Taoiseach on 30/06/1981.

In late May 1981, I received a demand from the Revenue Commissioners for IR£230,000 VAT belonging to Carpetdrome. With the benefit of hindsight, this demand was generated by the four-year draft accounts prepared by Tom Cullen, which I knew nothing about at the time. On the 23rd May, I went with Paul Jackson to Gaynor Tuffy's offices, where we met Mr Pat Tuffy. Mr Tuffy said Carpetdrome was going into liquidation and asked if I knew what a statement of affairs was. I replied that I did, and I was asked to furnish him with the information for one, together with £700 for fees. The statement of affairs was later prepared in front of me by Mr Tuffy when I brought over the information.

Mr Tuffy said that a meeting of creditors had been convened for the 3rd June and that he would place the advertisement, inviting creditors to make a claim, in the 'Evening Press' for the last Friday in May 1981.

The meeting went ahead at 10 am in the Sunnybank Hotel on Botanic Road in Glasnevin and was attended by only two creditors' representatives apart from myself. The Carpetdrome was indebted to Carpetdrive-In as a result of all the transfers, so I represented Carpetdrive-In. Before the meeting commenced, Paul Jackson succeeded in satisfying the other two creditors that their claims would be met, and they left. The creditors' meeting then went through the appointment of Mr Harding as liquidator. Mr Harding was put forward as a suitable person for the liquidator by Mr Tuffy. One other person who hoped to be appointed liquidator failed in his endeavours. The final attendance at the creditors' meeting was Paul Jackson, Pat Tuffy, Mr Harding, and me.

The statement of affairs presented to the meeting was an attenuated document giving stocks of IR£3,000, total assets of IR£6,000, and liabilities of almost £500,000, most of which was due to the Revenue

Commissioners. I gave Mr Harding a Carpetdrive-In cheque for IR£3,000 for the stock.

On 3rd June 1981, I took the Carpetdrome books to a warehouse in Benburb Street after the creditors' meeting. It took three journeys in an estate car to move the books.

On 16th June 1981, the Revenue raided the North Circular Road premises and seized most of the books, records, and documents of the Carpetdrive-In. The raid was led by Mr Thomas Tuite, who identified himself as from the Revenue's Special Investigation Branch. He was assisted by two or three other Revenue officials. As the Revenue had taken the books of Carpetdrive-In and was intent on holding on to them, I had no choice but to go to the Special Investigations Offices in Setanta House in order to examine Carpetdrive-In's books. After several visits to Setanta House, Matt Kelly ordered me to stay away. By that stage, I had extracted enough information to set up another set of books.

On Tuesday, 30th June 1981, Dr Garret Fitzgerald was voted in as Taoiseach. A very short time afterwards, a solicitor, whom I knew personally, tipped me off that he had heard from sources in the law library that a major case was being prepared around the affairs of Carpetdrome. A short time after this, I attended a midnight meeting in the home of Matthew Kelly, where he told me that the transfer of assets from Carpetdrome to Carpetdrive-In had backfired and that there was going to be a court case about it. Matthew Kelly said to me that I had better get offside.

He put a number of propositions to me. The first was that I should go on the beer and then have myself signed into St John of God's. The second was that I should have myself signed into a psychiatric institution or mental home. By doing either of these, I would render myself unreliable as a witness. The third proposition was that I should get out of the country. A few days later, I travelled to London and went to a house in St John's Wood, where I had stayed the previous year while attending the 1980 FA CUP final. I stayed there for two weeks. The plan was that I would stay in West London until I got a job and got myself sorted out.

When in London, I got the Irish Independent each day. On Wednesday, 29th July 1981, I found a report in the newspaper concerning the appointment of a liquidator to Kelly's Carpetdrome in the High Court on the previous day, Tuesday, 28th July 1981. Apparently, the Revenue Commissioners sought to overthrow Mr Harding's appointment as liquidator and to have him replaced with their own nominee. The Revenue made serious allegations of fraud. The presiding judge, Mr Herbert McWilliam, made an order appointing Mr Patrick Byrne as the official liquidator, thereby making him an officer of the court. Mr Byrne was a partner in Coopers & Lybrand Chartered Accountants.

Patrick Joseph Byrne is a member of one of Ireland's most famous political families. He was first elected as a TD in 1956 for the constituency of Dublin North East as an Independent. The seat became vacant upon the death of his father, Alfred Byrne. In a head-to-head contest, he defeated Charles Haughey by 17,000 votes to 12,000 votes. This was Charles Haughey's third unsuccessful attempt to be elected a TD. Byrne was re-elected as TD in the 1957 general election, this time as a Fine Gael TD. He held office until 1969. Both his brothers, Thomas Byrne and A.P. Byrne, were also TDs. Alfred Byrne is Dublin's most famous Lord Mayor. As well as being Lord Mayor of Dublin, Alfred Byrne was a councillor, a TD, and an MP in the Westminster Parliament between 1915 and 1918.

Following the report of the appointment of Mr Byrne as liquidator in the Irish Independent. I decided to return to Dublin after two weeks spent in West London. Mr Byrne's appointment changed the mood in Carpetdrive-In, and to my surprise, I was not pressurised to return to London, so I continued working as if nothing had happened. I explained my absence as being on vacation. In August 1981, Mr Byrne arrived at the premises with members of his staff and introduced himself as the liquidator of Carpetdrome to Paul Jackson and asked for the Carpetdrome's books. Paul Jackson said that he didn't have any books belonging to the Carpetdrome, and Mr Byrne went away. I was on the premises, in my office, and did not meet the liquidator.

The appointment of Mr Byrne as the liquidator by the High Court followed from the financial troubles of the Carpetdrome, which were all self-inflicted. It is a common complaint of the Kelly brothers, which is aired in the media, that their family origins in Dublin's north inner city had prevented them from entering third-level education, and that if they had gone to a business school, they would not have got into financial difficulty. This was a load of nonsense. As someone who went to a business school, I was the one who learnt from them, rather than them learning something from me.

On 14th October 1981, the liquidator swore an affidavit. This affidavit formed the basis of the liquidator's case against the Kellys. In the affidavit, Byrne said, *"It has become very clear to me that the circumstances in which the company ceased to trade on 28th February 1981 gave rise to serious implications of fraud on the part of the company. I believe that this company was run down, its assets divested from it and finally resolved to be wound up as part of a carefully planned scheme to defraud the State as the one major creditor left unpaid."*

The purpose of the affidavit was to freeze the assets of the Carpetdrive-In pending a full trial at a later date. If the application had been successful, the Carpetdrive-In business would have been closed down immediately. It then became necessary for the survival of the Carpetdrive-In to lodge a replying affidavit in order to challenge the liquidator's allegations. I then came under intense pressure from the Kellys to make a sworn affidavit. I refused, and the following day, I got a visit from Michael Deighan, who was wearing a raincoat and told me that he had a gun in his pocket and that he would use it if I didn't do the affidavit. He then put his hand in his pocket, and the outline of a gun began to appear, and he then left the office. Needless to say, the affidavit was prepared, sworn, and lodged. The affidavit was successful in preventing the liquidator from obtaining a freezing order. It was hoped that this would delay the case from being heard for two years, due to the backlog of High Court cases. It failed in this objective, as a date for a full trial was set for April 1982.

There had long been an association between the Kelly and Hutch families. Both families came from Dublin's north inner-city. Gerard Hutch's brother, Johnny, worked in the Carpetdrome as a warehouseman in charge of the laughing gear. The laughing gear is a term used in the carpet trade to describe the equipment used to rack rolls of carpet. Also, the Moncks' other two brothers, Paddy and Eddy, both fitted carpets for the Carpetdrome. Paddy and Eddy were both regular visitors to my office, where they presented subcontractors' bills for fitting carpets. As they weren't experienced carpet fitters, they provided backup when the store was busy. They usually only fitted felt back carpets in bedrooms.

Also, there was a theft of carpets from the warehouse around this time. A suspect was interrogated with the barrel of a shotgun being shoved down his throat, and the culprit was named. Shortly afterwards, the culprit was kneecapped on Dollymount Strand. The culprit was a brother-in-law of one of the Kelly brothers, and no mercy was shown even to a relative. It was Eamon Kelly himself who told me about this.

Before Christmas 1981, the liquidator of Kelly's Carpetdrome appealed an assessment raised by the Revenue Commissioners for unpaid taxes. The hearing took place before the Appeal Commissioners in St Stephen's Green. I gave evidence in the hearing for the liquidator. The result of the hearing was a determination of Carpetdrome's final tax liability for all taxes, interest, and penalties at IR£2,226,000, a very large sum back then.

The assessment for taxes came after a lot of fieldwork from the Revenue Commissioners. There were only two members of Coopers and Lybrand's staff involved in the liquidation. Patrick Byrne, the liquidator, and his assistant, Ernest Burden. They were supplemented by work carried out by Revenue Officials from the Special Investigations Division based in Setanta House, Nassau Street. The Revenue staff were supervised by Mr Thomas Tuite, an inspector of taxes. As a result of this, Coopers and Lybrand only deployed two of their staff to cut down on costs. This was a good strategy, as the possibility of the liquidator failing to collect anything for the State was quite high, and I have no doubt that Coopers and Lybrand's costs were guaranteed by the State. Also put at the disposal of the liquidator were the Revenue's legal team of Mr Richard Cooke SC and his son, Mr John Cooke SC. These barristers represented the Revenue Commissioners in all their major court cases. They were assisted by Mr Peter Kelly, BL, as Junior Counsel.

Early in the spring of 1982, the liquidator issued a High Court summons against Monck Properties, Kelly's Carpetdrive-In Ltd, Matthew Kelly, Eamon Kelly, Thomas Kelly, and Paul Jackson. A trial date was set for Tuesday, 20th April 1982. The liquidator sought a declaration that the scheme purporting to transfer the assets of Carpetdrome between October 1980 and June 1981 was a fraud on the creditors of Carpetdrome. He also sought an order setting aside the scheme and transfer and directing the retransfer of the assets to him. He also sought a declaration that all properties in the name of Monck Properties were purchased with money belonging to Carpetdrome and are held in trust for that company.

The week before the trial commenced, an informal meeting took place on the main floor of the carpet department. Eamon Kelly, Paul Jackson, Thomas Kelly, and Michael Deighan were in a huddle. I joined them while they were waiting for a phone call. A meeting was taking place between Matt Kelly and the liquidator. Matt Kelly was offering IR£1,000,000 to settle the case. It was mentioned that an intervention from Haughey would swing it, and hopes were very high for an acceptance of the offer. The offer was rejected, leading to last-minute efforts to prepare for the case. I remember attending the offices of George D Fottrell Solicitors on the Sunday evening preceding the start of the trial. I remember Fergal Gaynor, Matt Kelly, and James Salafia BL being at this meeting. The meeting went on until 11.30 pm, and Matt Kelly became very agitated. That night, Mr Richard Cooke's house in Clonskeagh was fire bombed. A seventy-year-old man and his wife were subjected to a fire bomb attack.

On Monday morning, Matt Kelly came into my office and denied that the attack had anything to do with him. At 11.00 pm on Tuesday, 20th April, the trial commenced. I was standing at the back of the court when the judge came out.

Eamon Kelly, who was standing right behind me, muttered, "Oh no, not Costello."

So, Mr Justice Costello was assigned the case by the president of the High Court. The Irish State had given the case to its most senior judge. Before becoming a High Court judge, Declan Costello had served as attorney general between 1973 and 1977. He was also the son of Ireland's first attorney general following independence, John A Costello. John A Costello was Taoiseach in 1948 and again in 1954. He is better known today as *'The Reluctant Taoiseach'* because he was a compromise candidate when Richard Mulcahy had to step down, as leader of Fine Gael, in order to form an interparty coalition government. The Costellos are the only father and son to hold the office of attorney general in the history of the Irish State.

Ronan Fanning, professor of modern history at University College Dublin, wrote an obituary on Declan Costello for the Sunday Independent in June 2011. Fanning said, *"His outstanding achievement was the successful conduct of the Irish government's case against the UK before the European Court of Human Rights in regard to the torture of prisoners in the North when he was acclaimed as having wiped the floor with his British counterpart."*

Former Taoiseach Liam Cosgrave publicly declared in 2009, "He was an outstanding Attorney General and I never found him wrong on anything."

Declan Costello was also the outstanding authority on Copyright and Patent law in Ireland. Because of this, his judgements on Patent and Copyright cases were fully reported in British Law Journals. Declan Costello was our equivalent of the famous British Judge, Lord Denning.

I had already been subpoenaed by the liquidator. The trial lasted only four days and was settled on Friday, 23rd April 1982. The liquidator got relief for his claim through a consenting order, with the agreement of Matt Kelly and Eamon Kelly, whereby the assets and liabilities of Monck Properties were aggregated with those of Carpetdrome. This meant that Monck Properties became a wholly owned subsidiary of Carpetdrome, thus giving the liquidator control over the property company. Under the arrangement, Carpetdrive-In was allowed to continue to trade for the remainder of its lease, which was advantageous to the liquidator as Carpetdrive-In was paying Monck Properties IR£3,000 per week in rent.

During the trial, Matt Kelly asked for an adjournment while negotiations were going on to try to settle the case. Mr Justice Costello refused the request, saying that the case was in the public interest and must continue uninterrupted. Mr Niall Fennelly SC, who was representing Carpetdrive-In and its directors, turned around to me and said that what Judge Costello had just said was a hint from the bench that if the case was not settled, it was going to the guards. Mr Fennelly then said that I should use all my influence to get the case settled, and I said that I would do my best. The case was settled, and I was not called to give evidence. The case received widespread publicity in the media, and, in particular, in the newspapers. The publicity had a negative effect on the Carpetdrive-In trade in carpets, and the allegations of fraud made it almost impossible to get insurance cover. The only insurance company that would take on the risk of a fire was Lloyds of London, and at a very high premium. So, the business was placed with Lloyds, and only a fraction of the premium was ever paid.

In May 1982, with the court case out of the way, I started to concentrate on the financial affairs of Carpetdrive-In. Preparations for the April court case were a distraction, and the books of Carpetdrive-In were not up to date. It took me until the end of May to get things up to date. I asked Paul Jackson to help me organise a stock take, which he duly obliged. The result of the stock take was IR£130,000. This was a very low figure against supply creditors of IR£500,000 and revenue debts of IR£130,000. As Carpetdrive-In had very few other assets, this was a very serious situation, and the company was grossly insolvent.

After the court case, Carpetdrive-In paid the liquidator the weekly rent of IR£3,000 only once and was now in arrears for rent of IR£9,000 at least. I cast my mind back to July 1981, when four large sums, IR£12,000, IR£12,000, IR£10,000, and IR£8,000, were lodged to the Carpetdrive-In current account on four consecutive days. These sums did not arise from normal sales. Eamon Kelly told me to put these amounts down as directors' loans. As there were three directors, I allocated one of the three larger amounts to each of them as directors' loans. This left the fourth sum of IR£8,000 to be accounted for. I put down the IR£8,000 as a loan from myself. A couple of weeks later, I realised the serious error of judgement I had made, and I transferred the IR£8,000 to a suspense account. It was company policy with the Kellys that any unaccounted money was treated as a loan of some description.

Looking back, with the benefit of hindsight, it is obvious that the practice of a second set of sales books was in operation in Carpetdrive-In, that too much unrecorded sales had been diverted, and that the four separate large lodgements were excessive unrecorded sales being recycled. Therefore, I should have put all four amounts into a suspense account. It also looks as if the persistent use of unrecorded sales had produced another insolvency and that the revenue liability was grossly understated, as I had not taken into account the impact of the unrecorded sales in calculating the Carpetdrive-In's VAT liability. So, it looks as if Carpetdrive-In was the final instalment of a *Kelly's Carpet Carry On* saga. The other two preceding episodes were Kelly's Carpet Supermarket (in liquidation) and Kelly's Carpetdrome (in liquidation). Carpetdrive-In was now on borrowed time.

At or around this time, one of the carpet salesmen, with whom I was friendly, confided in me that he was coming under intense pressure from the guards. Apparently, he leased a car in his name on the instructions of Eamon Kelly. The car was used in connection with a murder in Crumlin. Gerard Morgan (15) was shot dead as he came to the front door of his family home at 22 Lismore Road, Crumlin, on 26th May 1982. It is believed that his older brother, Alan Morgan (17), was the intended target.

The killing was connected to an armed robbery carried out by the Hutch gang in Drumcondra several weeks earlier that netted the gang the equivalent of €80,000. But one robber, Michael McDonnell, hid his share of the loot in his garden in Crumlin, and it was found by a teenage pal of Gerard Morgan, who told Gerard Morgan about it. The two teenage boys then spent some of the stolen loot. Gerard Morgan told his older brother, Alan Morgan, about the money. Alan Morgan and a friend then stole the remainder of the loot. The Hutch gang soon identified the suspects and began putting pressure on Alan Morgan and the other suspects. The gang visited the Morgan house at one stage, and weeks later, Gerard Morgan was shot dead when a bullet was fired through the front door, killing him instantly.

Despite the guards having a strong case against Eamon Kelly for the possession of a firearm with the intention to endanger life, Eamon Kelly was never charged because the Director of Prosecutions ruled that there was insufficient evidence. The killing of Gerard Morgan, a fifteen-year-old boy, shocked the public, making it a new low in Ireland.

On Friday, 4th June 1982, Eamon Kelly was having lunch in Foley's Coffee shop on the North Circular Road, directly opposite the Carpetdrive-In, with Jimmy Flynn, a senior member of the Official IRA. When they finished lunch, a member of staff gave Flynn a lift to Cusack's Bar on North Strand Road in Ballybough. There was a car parked outside Cusack's Bar, which was behind Croke Park, and Flynn went into the bar and identified himself to the barman, who handed him a set of keys. Flynn left the bar immediately and went over to the driver's door of the car parked outside the bar. As he was putting the key into the lock, a motorcycle with a pillion passenger approached the car and pulled up beside Flynn. The pillion passenger then pulled out a gun and shot Jimmy Flynn dead, and the motorcycle then went off.

It was around this time that another salesman confided in me that Eamon Kelly had pressurised the salesman to lease a car in his own name. This car was then used in the murder of Jimmy Flynn. I assume that the leased car was the car that Flynn was attempting to open when he was shot dead. This was a different salesman from the salesman who leased the car used in the murder of Gerard Morgan in Crumlin the previous May. The salesman who leased the car used in the Flynn murder also came under enormous pressure from the guards to name Eamon Kelly.

One could feel the tension in the Carpetdrive-In the following week. There were visits from members of the Workers' Party looking for Eamon Kelly. On one occasion, I recognised Sean Garland, the former Adjutant General of the Official IRA and leader of the Workers' Party from 1998 to 2008, who was looking for Eamon Kelly. Garland and his associates looked very tense, as they were very anxious to find out what was going on. However, as Eamon Kelly had made himself scarce, this had made the situation worse. The carpet business was already a front for organised crime, but now, it was becoming a front for murder.

The week commencing Monday, 7th June 1982, was the last week that the Carpetdrive-In traded. I had three conversations with Matt Kelly that week when it was mentioned that Carpetdrive-In was going to be burned down, once on the company premises, then in the Midland Hotel, Dominic Street, and finally in the Shelbourne Hotel. I got the impression that the fire would be on Sunday, 13th June, as Meat Loaf was performing a concert in Dalymount Park, and this would provide a cover for the fire. The racks in the centre of the sales floor were dismantled, and the carpet rolls were laid on the floor right up the centre of the sales floor, so that they would form a conveyor belt for the fire to move from one end of the building to the other. The expensive Axminster wool carpets were removed from the sales floor and replaced with cheaper synthetic carpets with felt backs, which were highly inflammable. The overall level of carpet rolls was significantly reduced, but enough stock was left to ensure that the fire would take hold of the building.

On Monday, 14th June, I came to work as normal. What I thought might have happened the previous night did not happen. I left the premises around 7 pm and went into Mooney's bar at Doyle's Corner to watch the World Cup football. The match that was on that evening was Brazil versus the USSR. During the middle of the second half, somebody came into the bar off the street and shouted that the carpet store was up in flames. So that was it, and it was all over.

CHAPTER 4

THE RECKONING

"In this life there are three things one cannot hide. The first is the sun, the second is the moon and the third is the truth."
—Buddha, 400 BC.

The fire destroyed the Carpetdrive-In premises. It also caused major disruption to the North Circular Road and to Doyles Corner. A section of the North Circular Road had to be cordoned off, with traffic being diverted for a week. This was to facilitate engineers checking out adjacent buildings for structural damage. After the inspection, no such damage was found, and the public regained access to the area.

Approximately 50 people lost their jobs. As no PAYE/PRSI had been paid by Carpetdrive-In, staff were not entitled to social welfare payments. The soft furnishings and curtain business survived the fire. This business was run by George Allis, who had left Penny's store in Mary Street and joined Carpetdrome as a soft furnishings buyer in 1978. Matt Kelly found this business troublesome, so in 1981, George Allis took over the business from the Kellys, purchasing the stock and paying them rent. Up to the fire, I had done the books for his business. After the fire, he gave me a full-time job, combining sales with administration. I was very thankful for this, as the whiff of scandal coming from the fire and the court case made it almost impossible to get another job.

George Allis's business had survived the fire, with the shop frontage being on the North Circular Road and adjacent to other retail premises. However, the back of the shop was extended into the internal car park and was destroyed in the fire, causing substantial loss of stock. The remainder of the stock was contaminated by smoke damage, and so he held a fire salvage sale. So, we opened on Sundays to facilitate this sale.

The first Sunday we opened, we got an unexpected visitor. Patrick Byrne, the liquidator, had just arrived back from his annual holiday in Greece that morning. Upon boarding the aircraft full of returning holiday makers, the plane was a buzz of conversations about the fire on the carpet premises. Being in the dark, he was taken aback by what he heard. Upon his arrival at Dublin Airport, he went back to his Donnybrook home. He then made the trip to Phibsborough and came into the curtain shop where I greeted him. So, I took him around to Phibsborough shopping centre. We then made our way onto the roof of the shopping centre, which acted as a car park. From here, we had a grandstand view of the burnt-out shell of the carpet store. It wasn't a pretty sight, with the roof gone and all the mangled steel, which was once the structure of the carpet store.

Byrne looked visibly shaken. He just wasn't looking at the destruction fire causes; he was looking at the work of organised crime, and he knew it. We then left without saying much more, and this reminded me of the Latin phrase *'Res Ipsa Loquitor,'* which translates as, *'The thing speaks for itself.'*

The aftermath of the fire did not free me from the clutches of the Kellys. They wanted me to work on the preparation of their insurance claim. With all the records destroyed in the fire, I had no appetite for this task, and hence, I did not cooperate. Then, as I found the four tyres of my car slashed, I got the message. An office was set up in the old State Cinema for me to work in. The cinema was not in use and was owned by Des Kelly. I worked on the insurance claim as documents became available.

1983 arrived as sure as night follows day. The new year brought with it newspaper reports that the liquidator was applying to the High Court for permission to take a fresh case against the Kellys. The fire had caused the destruction of the Carpetdrive-In premises, the major property in the Monck Properties portfolio. This property had not been adequately insured, as only a fraction of the premium had been paid. Lloyds, the insurers, were bound to vigorously challenge any claim with the serious allegations of fraud surrounding the case. Other Kelly properties in the city centre were either heavily mortgaged or had short leases. Despite winning the 1982 High Court case, the liquidator had gained little or nothing. This was a point not lost on Judge Declan Costello, so when approving the settlement, he asked counsel for the liquidator if they had received enough.

In May 1983, I was subpoenaed, and the case opened again before Mr Justice Declan Costello in the High Court on Monday, 21st June

1983. This time, the action brought by the liquidator against Matt Kelly and Eamon Kelly was taken under *Section 297* of the *Companies Act 1963*. This section deals with fraudulent trading, and it says that the relief available to the plaintiff is liability for the total debts of the company without limitation of liability against the directors of the company and anyone else who knowingly participated in the fraud. The director of public prosecutions can also take an action, under the same section, for fraudulent trading, and if successful, the sanction is a term of imprisonment.

Although the case taken by the liquidator was a civil case, a *Section 297* case is known in the legal world as a quasi-criminal one. Normally, civil cases are decided on the balance of probability, and in criminal cases, the burden of proof is beyond a reasonable doubt. In a *Section 297* application, the burden of proof shifts from the balance of probability towards beyond a reasonable doubt. This is sort of a halfway house between a civil case and a criminal case. For this reason, very few cases are taken under *Section 297* of the Companies Act.

The case taken by Byrne, in 1982, was a civil case alleging breach of trust, alleging that vast sums of money were taken out of Carpetdrome and transferred into Monck Properties and used to accumulate a property portfolio. The case was settled in the middle of the 1982 hearing, when Matt Kelly agreed to transfer Monck Properties to the liquidator in settlement of his claim. To give effect to this arrangement, Justice Costello made an aggregating order combining the assets and liabilities of Carpetdrome with those of Monck. In effect, Monck

Properties became a subsidiary of Carpetdrome, its parent. However, this relief proved to be inadequate, and hence we were all back in court.

The first couple of days were a replay of last year's case. The liquidator presented his case and then called his main witnesses, who were mainly tax officials. Matt Kelly and Eamon Kelly were the respondents, and the liquidator sought to make the two brothers personally liable for the debts of both Kellys Carpetdrome Ltd. and Monk Properties Ltd. The Revenue Commissioners' regular legal team represented the liquidator. They were led by Mr Richard Cooke SC, his son, Mr John Cooke SC, and Mr Peter Kelly BL. The Kellys failed to obtain legal representation due to their reputation. The firebombing of Mr Richard Cooke's house the previous year did not help. So, Matthew Kelly defended himself as he was entitled to do. Eamon Kelly adopted his brother's defence.

Because Matt Kelly had no legal representation, he relied heavily on an associate, Michael Deighan, for advice. Michael Deighan was from the East Wall suburb in Dublin. He had a criminal conviction for possession of IR£2,000 worth of cigarettes in 1958. This was the value of a semi-detached house back in those days. He subsequently went to America and was involved in organised crime, becoming a gangster's bodyguard in Chicago. Due to his involvement in crime in America, he was deported and returned to Ireland in the early 1960s. He was caught on the roof of the Bank of Ireland in Talbot Street while trying to break into the bank, for which he received a prison sentence. While in prison, he told me that he shared a cell with Dr Paul Singer of Shanahan stamp fame. Dr Singer was preparing his own defence, and for that purpose, he was consulting law books. He introduced Deighan to the study of law, which he pursued up to the time I met him. Deighan had a small dwelling and a farm of about seven acres in St Margaret's in the north county, Dublin. I visited the farm as part of the stock taking exercise I took in 1982, as rolls of carpets were stored in a premises on the farm. Deighan was released from prison, without fully serving his sentence, by the government in 1969. The purpose of his release was to organise the criminal fraternity into a group that would carry out bank robberies to raise funds to purchase guns for the defence of nationalists from loyalist attacks in Northern Ireland.

This group were joined by members of the IRA who were unhappy with the IRA's lack of action. A former member of this group explained to me in 1982 that the proceeds of the bank robberies were split three ways: one-third to the bosses who supplied the guns, another third to those who carried out the robbery, and the remainder went north. These robberies came to an end in April 1970, when Garda Fallon was shot dead in Smithfield while answering a call to a robbery in the Allied Irish Bank branch on Arran Quay. The weapon used to murder Garda Fallon was traced to an importation of arms organised by a government minister.

Deighan came to national prominence when he was busted by the Sunday World newspaper for holding interviews in the Gresham Hotel for recruiting young females for a career in modelling. The real purpose of the interview was to offer them a role in pornographic films. Deighan lost a subsequent action against the Sunday World for libel in 1982. He drove around town in a red Mustang car and mostly wore a raincoat like the American actor and detective, Columbo. Deighan helped out other criminals in preparing Habeas Corpus applications, along with other legal matters, and became a type of godfather figure, combining his criminal career with his knowledge of the law.

So, Deighan sat behind Matt Kelly in the High Court on the right side of the courtroom, which is traditionally the side of the room where respondents sat. On one occasion that week, he sat beside me. Matt Kelly was on his feet directly in front of us. I noticed at one point that Judge Costello turned away from Kelly and looked towards Richard and John Cooke. Judge Costello then put his hand on the left-hand side of his face, clearly covering his left eye. To me, this was a signal of his disapproval of Deighan in court. As Deighan sat behind Matt Kelly, he began prompting Kelly as Kelly was cross-examining Thomas Tuite, the inspector of taxes. Tuite complained to the judge that these prompts were distracting him when replying to Kelly's questions. The judge then issued a warning to everybody else in court to remain silent. Prior to Deighan's arrival, he had no difficulty in facing Matt Kelly, the same way he had focused on the Cookes when they were addressing the judge.

Decan Costello was attorney general between March 1973 and May 1977. As the office of the director of public prosecutions was not established until January 1975, the office of the attorney general was responsible for state prosecutions. I am sure that Declan Costello became well acquainted with Deighan between March 1973 and December 1975.

The case was held in a chamber on the first floor of the Four Courts. This is up the stairs on the right-hand side of the Round Hall. This floor contains two courtrooms. The one furthest from the top of the stairs was the room where the Kelly Case was at a hearing before Mr Justice Costello. In the room nearest the top of the stairs, another case was being heard by Miss Justice Majella Carroll. The case that she was hearing was taken by businessman James Mansfield against an insurance company. Mansfield was claiming for a container full of machine parts that were destroyed following a hijacking by the Provisional IRA north of the border; the insurers had refused to pay out, contesting the bona fides of the claim. As I had seen James Mansfield and Matt Kelly in the company together on several occasions, I thought it ironic that both of them should be at the centre of two high-profile High Court cases on the same floor and next door to each other at the same time.

On Friday morning, I walked up the stairs heading towards the courtroom. I was approached by Matt Kelly, who wanted me to say that *'proper books of account were kept by the Carpetdrome,'* when, in fact, there was no nominal ledger and no stock records, and no stock-taking ever took place. As a result of this, there were no final accounts, such as a profit & loss account and a balance sheet. I replied that I would be under oath and that I could not comply with his request.

Kelly then said, "You are either with me or against me," and added, "The other crowd tell lies."

The meeting then broke up, and both of us went into the courtroom. The liquidator began to get through his list of witnesses. It seemed like the less important the witness, the shorter the time spent in the witness box, and this is what happened this day.

On Friday afternoon, it became apparent that I would be called next by the liquidator's legal team, as they had just finished with Kelly's accountant, Fergal Gaynor. Matt Kelly sensed this and called for a short adjournment at 3.00 pm, which was granted by the judge. So, we left the courtroom and went out to the corridor. Deighan came over to me and told me to give a girl who worked in Bradshaw solicitors a lift home. I replied that I had no car with me, and then Deighan told me to *'get out'* in a threatening manner. I left the Four Courts in haste.

That weekend, I felt very unsettled after being interfered with by Matt Kelly in the morning, and later that afternoon, being ordered out of court by Michael Deighan. I had been pressurised by Matt Kelly to commit perjury. I had no doubt that Mr Justice Costello would refer the case to the DPP at the end of the trial. I had no choice but to come clean and tell the truth. So, I started preparing a statement from the commencement of employment right up to the previous Friday.

On Monday morning, I received a phone call from Hubert Donnelly, a pal of mine. He said that Michael Deighan had just contacted him by phone. Deighan asked Donnelly to ring me with a message to attend a meeting in a derelict warehouse in Prussia Street for discussions about the court case before the case resumes in the High

Court. I told Donnelly to tell Deighan, if he rang back, that I was on my way over.

This didn't sound too healthy to me, so I headed over to the northside. Instead of going to Prussia Street, I went to Mountjoy Garda Station and brought the fifteen-page statement along with me. I went to Mountjoy Garda Station, as my father had sold his residential newsagent's business adjacent to the station two years earlier, and as a result of this, I was well acquainted with the serving guards in that station. There, I was met by Sargent Liam Cohen, who took me into the interview room. I explained to him what was going on, and he read my statement. When he finished reading the statement, he got me to sign it at the end of the statement. He also marked the two paragraphs where I had made allegations against both Kelly and Deighan regarding interference outside the courtroom last Friday. So, I put my signature opposite each paragraph. He told me to stay where I was until he came back. It was now 10.30 am, and he did not return until 1.30 pm. It later transpired that he contacted his Inspector Dick Walsh, and they went to the Bridewell to see their superintendent. When the three of them got together, they went over to see the Director of Public Prosecutions, Eamonn Barnes, in person. The DPP then directed the detectives to go back to Mountjoy Garda station and bring me down to the Four Courts.

We arrived in the High Court at 2.30 pm. Mr Justice Costello then came into the court. Detective Sargent Liam Cohen outlined the events that had taken place that morning and, in particular, the direction from the DPP. I was then sworn in and took my seat in the witness box. I started to give evidence, and Judge Costello stopped me to make an announcement that he was now hearing evidence for the charge of criminal contempt of court. He also made a direction that the liquidator's barristers should act for the DPP as in a criminal prosecution. Judge Costello then directed the guard in court to arrest both Kelly and Deighan. Matt Kelly kept his cool and remained in the court. However, Deighan fled the court but was apprehended outside the courtroom in the Round Hall. It was several minutes before he was brought back into the court under arrest. The reason for the delay was that he had fouled himself, and the detectives had to take him to a nearby toilet to clean himself. I noticed from the witness box that Eileen Hogg, who had preceded me in the Carpetdrome, was present in court.

As it became apparent that I had defected to the liquidator and, hence, became hostile to the Kellys, she was ushered out of court by Niall Mulvihill. It was high drama in the High Court. So, a trial within a trial was set in motion. The following Thursday was set for the full trial of criminal contempt of court. The defendants asked for the trial to be held the following week. This application was refused on the grounds that I was threatened and that I was in fear for my life. An application for bail by Kelly and Deighan was refused after Liam Cohen objected on the grounds that I would be interfered with by the defendants. The court adjourned at 4 pm. Before he adjourned, Mr Justice Costello said to me that I had made it clear to him that I was in fear of my life and then asked me if I could come to court tomorrow. I replied that I would come to court tomorrow, and then the judge said that if I had any doubt that I might not be able to attend court tomorrow, he was prepared to continue hearing my evidence even if the court had to sit through the night.

I left the Four Courts under Garda escort, and the guards brought me over to the Bridewell Garda Station. They stayed with me until my official escort arrived. After an hour, two detectives arrived at the Bridewell. Detective Sargent Jude Murphy and Detective Garda Mick Drew introduced themselves to me. They told me Jude Murphy was shot in November 1972, in the Mater Hospital, following an unsuccessful attempt by the Provisional IRA to free Sean McStiofain while being treated after several days on hunger strike. Two members of the Provisional IRA unit were dressed as priests. I later discovered that they were delayed due to their superiors organising a bulletproof car. There was only one bulletproof car in the State, and that car belonged to the British Embassy. It was summertime, and the ambassador was on holiday, so the guards borrowed the bulletproof car from the British Government. They used this car as my escort for about two weeks until the ambassador returned from abroad. As well as having a bulletproof car, the guards had a Uzi, a submachine gun with six magazines, each containing 28 bullets. An executive-type briefcase housed the submachine gun and the six magazines when not in use. They also carried a very powerful Magnum .38 handgun, which was loaded, and they also had a pouch carrying spare ammunition strapped either to their waist or to their calf.

Both detectives were members of the elite Garda Special Task Force. We left the Bridewell in the bulletproof car, and they drove me to where my car was parked. We found the car punctured, so we changed the wheel. Then we headed for home, which was a three-bedroom semi-detached house with a garage. On the way home, the guards followed me in the bulletproof car. Tea-time traffic was heavy, and I spotted a vendor selling newspapers. He had a bundle of the *Evening Press* newspapers tucked under his arm. I was going to pull up and buy a newspaper, but then I noticed the headline *'High Court Sensation,'* so I said to myself, *"Why bother buying a newspaper? Sure, I am the news."*

The case dominated the newspapers for the whole week. Protection was not confined to me alone. Everybody connected with the liquidator's case had to get Garda protection. This included the liquidator and his assistant, Mr Tuite and his assistants, and the liquidator's legal team. Even Mr Justice Costello was the recipient of Garda protection. All this protection was unarmed and took the form of security on their houses, bearing in mind the firebomb attack on Mr Richard Cooke's house a year earlier.

When I arrived home, the garage door was open, and there were two uniformed guards on duty. I had some explaining to do to my mother, who, I can assure you, was not impressed. That evening was busy with guards coming and going. Jude Murphy and Mick Drew were replaced by two younger detectives. It was a hot day, and the new detectives and I adjourned to the Glenside Bar in Churchtown for a few light refreshments. When I returned home at midnight, my mother was having a cup of tea with a senior detective. She introduced me to Chief Superintendent Ned Ryan and then left us together, having gone to bed. Ned Ryan was based in Crumlin Garda Station and was the chief superintendent over Crumlin, Terenure, and Rathfarnham Stations. He was a high-profile senior Garda, having led the Garda investigation into the Sallins train robbery. He was known as the *'Buffalo'* to the general public. The following day, my mother told me that Ryan himself had told her that he was under protection as a result of the threats he had received while investigating the train robbery.

The purpose of Chief Superintendent Ryan's visit was to warn me about a Provisional IRA mole within the Garda Special Detective Unit, which is more commonly referred to by the general public as the *Special Branch*. He advised me not to trust or get too friendly with the guards who would be protecting me. He said that Eamonn Kelly was a member of the Official IRA, something that I already knew. He said that senior guards were very concerned that the Provisional IRA mole would pass on information about my security detail to Eamonn Kelly because, obviously, Kelly was part of the wider IRA family. He strongly advised me never to discuss my future movements or arrangements with the detectives who were protecting me, as loose talk amongst detectives in Dublin Castle could be intercepted by the mole who could then pick out a weakness in my security detail and pass this on to Kelly.

Chief Superintendent Ryan said that while the identity of the mole was not known, senior Garda had no doubts about his or her existence. He said that the mole had been active for a considerable amount of time, but that they had been unable to pinpoint who was passing information on to the Provisional IRA. It would be difficult to identify the culprit out of a population of about 800 personnel. He asked me not to discuss this with the detectives who were protecting me, as these detectives didn't know about the mole's existence. I got the impression that very few people in the country knew about the mole's existence, and those who did know were advanced in their years, and that knowledge of the mole was confined to senior Garda and senior politicians. For the record, Garret Fitzgerald was Taoiseach, Dick Spring was Tánaiste, Michael Noonan was the minister for justice, Peter Sutherland was the attorney general, Eamonn Barnes was the director of public prosecutions, and Larry Wren was Garda commissioner. Chief Superintendent Ryan also advised me to keep changing my routes, even though I was under protection, in order to reduce the risk of an attack. After about an hour, he left.

Monday, 27th June, had been a very eventful day. I had avoided a suspicious meeting with Michael Deighan in a derelict warehouse in Prussia Street. I gave evidence in the High Court, resulting in the arrest of Michael Deighan and Matt Kelly, and I became the first person in the history of the Irish State to enter a witness protection programme. I had met two of the most high-profile Garda officers, and the existence of a Provisional IRA mole right at the heart of the Irish State's security apparatus was revealed to me.

Fair play to the guards who had acted very swiftly in organising my protection in getting the bulletproof car off the British Embassy and warning me about the threat of the Provisional IRA mole. I have to say that I was astonished that they told me about the mole, because at the time of writing, some forty years later, his existence remains a secret.

On Tuesday, 28th June, I drove to the Four Courts under escort. I stopped on the way to buy a newspaper. The case had made the front page of the *Irish Independent* with a headline *'Death Row Witness Puts Carpet King in Jail.'* I arrived in court at 11.00 pm. Mr Adrian Hardiman SC appeared in court for Matt Kelly and Michael Deighan. He made a couple of applications to the court in connection with the criminal contempt of court trial, which Mr Justice Costello dealt with. When Mr Hardiman was finished, Michael Deighan was removed from court and returned to Mountjoy Prison, as he was not a party to the Companies Act proceedings. I then returned to the witness box. Mr Justice Costello then asked me about my circumstances, and I told him that I was under protection. I think the judge was expecting me to say that I was on a witness protection programme; however, unfortunately, I gave a rather clumsy answer.

By an extraordinary coincidence, two Royal Ulster Constabulary detectives were attending the Mansfield case in the courtroom next door. They had been investigating Mansfield's claim against his insurers, which they did not consider bona fide for several years. The container of spare parts was hijacked and destroyed by the Provisional IRA, and the RUC officers were determined to prevent the Provisional IRA from getting a cut out of the claim. The two RUC officers were given armed protection from the Garda Special Task Force because they were witnesses in the Mansfield case. The RUC officers were very disappointed that the Dublin media ignored the Mansfield case and concentrated on the Kelly Carpets case. In the end, the two RUC officers threw in the towel and came into the courtroom next door to follow the Kelly Carpets case, as this was where all the action was taking place. This was all conveyed to me the following week by the Special Task Force detectives who were protecting the three of us.

Mr Richard Cooke SC then commenced examining me under the Companies Act. At this point, I had defected to the liquidator. Even though I had been subpoenaed by the liquidator, I was considered a hostile witness by the liquidator's lawyers and on the side of the Kellys. However, my defection changed all that. The evidence that I gave concerned the fraudulent trading by Carpetdrome: the two sets of books maintained by the Carpetdrome, the transfer of stock to Carpetdrive-In, the arson of the Carpetdrive-In premises, and the knee capping on Dollymount strand following a theft of carpets. When I mentioned the role of the accountancy firm Gaynor & Tuffy in the transfer of Carpetdrome business into Carpetdrive-In, Mr Richard Cooke asked the judge for permission to take a further *Section 297* application against the accountants. The judge immediately granted the application. After all that, the court adjourned for lunch at 1.00 pm. As I left the court, the court stenographer followed me. She then asked me if I was leaving the country when the case was over. I replied that I was going nowhere.

Over the lunch hour, I pondered whether I should tell Mr Justice Costello about Matt Kelly's payment to Haughey. The case had reached the stage where the atmosphere was very tense. This revelation would have been sensational and explosive and would have rocked the Irish State to its foundations. I could have changed the whole course of modern Irish history that afternoon, but I hesitated and chose not to do so. With the benefit of hindsight, I deeply regret that I did not tell the judge about the payment; I realise it was the biggest mistake of my life. I have no doubt that Mr Justice Costello, a former TD himself, would have sorted out the messing that goes on in this country and saved the taxpayer millions by avoiding the costs of future tribunals of inquiry. I am not so sure that the legal profession would have welcomed this.

At 2.00 pm, the court resumed, and I returned to the witness box. This time, I had to face cross-examination from my former employer, Matt Kelly, in person, as he was representing himself and was also under arrest. It was a dramatic experience, and Mr Justice Costello allowed proceedings to carry on until 5.00 pm. Normally, the High Court sits until 4.00 pm.

I returned to court on Thursday, 30th June, for the criminal contempt of court trial, which was a trial within a trial. I took the stand first, and I was cross-examined by Mr Adrian Hardiman SC on the evidence that I had given to the court on Monday. Mr Hardiman contested that the conversations that I had with Matt Kelly and Michael Deighan never took place on the previous Friday. These conversations were the basis of the criminal contempt of court charges. I stood my ground and was adamant that these events did take place. It was basically my word against theirs. The cross-examination lasted only thirty minutes, and I then withdrew from the witness box.

I was followed by a succession of witnesses, for the defence, who were out in the corridor outside the court last Friday at 3.00 pm, when Matt Kelly requested an adjournment. When these witnesses finished their evidence, counsel for the DPP and the defence started quoting UK cases on criminal contempt of court. One such case stuck out in my mind where somebody in the UK let off a stink bomb in court in order to force an adjournment! After hearing legal arguments from both sides, Mr Justice Costello delivered his verdict. He had decided to accept my evidence on the basis that I was a perfectly honest witness and also an accurate witness. He convicted Matt Kelly and Michael Deighan of criminal contempt of court and sentenced them to six months' imprisonment.

I had just made Irish legal history by becoming the first state witness to give evidence in a criminal trial, at the direction of the director of public prosecutions, while on a witness protection programme. On Friday, 1st July, the liquidator's case resumed. Closing submissions were made by the liquidator's barristers. Judge Costello then asked Eamon Kelly if he wanted to adopt his brother's defence, and he agreed to do so. Coming up to 1.00 pm, just before he adjourned, Mr Justice Costello declared that judgement would be delivered at 2.00 pm later that afternoon.

The court resumed at 2.00 pm, and the judge read out his judgement from a thirty-page document, which took him about forty-five minutes.

Matt Kelly and Eamon Kelly were made personally liable for the debts of Carpetdrome and Monk Properties without limitation of liability. As I expected, he referred the case to the DPP to consider criminal prosecutions. For that purpose, he ordered the liquidator to hand over his files to the DPP. Counsel for the liquidator, Mr John Cooke SC, asked for orders to be granted to give effect to the judgement. As the hearing concluded, the court broke up, and we awaited the next episode in the case, the *Section 297* proceedings against Gaynor & Tuffy.

I was astounded by Judge Costello having his judgement ready within an hour of the hearing finishing. I read the judgement a couple of months later. One would think from reading his judgement that he actually worked in the Carpetdrome—such was his grasp of what actually went on there. I think that Judge Costello had rendered an outstanding public service in his handling of the arrest of Kelly and Deighan, the trial within a trial, and the civil case itself, all in very dramatic circumstances. I felt that he never got the recognition that he was due. He was, without doubt, the most impressive person I had ever encountered in my entire life. He was in contact with the chief superintendent of the Special Detective Unit to voice his concerns over my safety, which was a wonderful gesture on his part. He checked out my safety to ensure that I had been properly looked after before he referred the case to the DPP. That is what a gentleman does.

CHAPTER 5

HAUGHEY OF KINSEALY

"Law is the art of hiding the politics behind a judgement."
—Brendan McGoldrick 2023.

I returned to work on the Monday after the case closed. My workplace was George Allis's fabric shop on the North Circular Road. I had been in touch with George over the previous week while the case was at hearing, and he was very supportive. He let me return to work, and the Garda Special Task Force car pulled up on the pavement outside the shop. He could have dismissed me, and I could not have blamed him. Fortunately, he did not dismiss me, as there was no State support for persons on a witness protection programme because, at that time, the State had not formalised witness protection programmes. At the time of writing, the same was the case, even after forty years. The best that the State could come up with was a protocol for the Special Detective Unit to follow when taking a witness into protection.

There was a cloud of secrecy in this country surrounding witness protection, and, in my opinion, this was due to my mentioning of Charles Haughey in my statement back in 1983 while under protection.

I believe that the Irish State refused to formalise the witness protection programme by introducing legislation in parliament to regulate the witness protection programme. Such statutory legislation would have provided an opportunity for me to make a claim against the State. As my witness protection programme was covered up, a claim taken against the Irish State would have undone this cover-up. Business carried on as normal, and the security did not deter customers from coming into the shop. One of the detectives stayed in the shop, and as the shop was quite large, most people thought that the detective was a customer.

Two weeks following the case, I went out for a long walk one evening and ended up in the Horse Show House in Ballsbridge. It was a warm evening, and a few drinks were welcome. I noticed that another four members of the Task Force appeared out of nowhere and joined the company. I did not realise it at the time, but those four other detectives were also part of my security detail and were operating as a shadow squad unknown to me. Also, that night, I bumped into a detective who introduced himself as a member of the Special Detective Unit, who was on duty on Thursday when the criminal contempt of court trial took place. He said that it took a ring of seventy armed detectives around the Four Courts to ensure that I got to court safely. Garda informers had indicated that there was no way that I would be giving evidence, and so the Garda allocated huge manpower to the case to make sure that I could give evidence. He told me that the Garda were determined to back the courts to the hilt. Looking back to that Thursday when I was in the witness box, Michael Deighan caught my eye and gave me a wink to acknowledge his surprise at my making it to court. The detective also told me that I passed very near to him in the Four Courts on that Thursday morning and that he would not have recognised me in the bar if it hadn't been for the security that he had spotted. He said that my appearance had changed dramatically since that Thursday morning. In other words, *the colour had returned to my cheeks*.

Mr Tuite, who was leading the Revenue investigation, got in touch with me. I attended his offices in Setanta Place, where he interviewed me over two days. I gave him a statement, which he said was going to be used in the forthcoming action against Gaynor & Tuffy. We discussed the recent case, and he said that he was very worried about his own personal safety. Mr Tuite also said that Mr Justice Costello was a person of outstanding intellectual ability, and whatever impression I made upon Mr Tuite, he seemed to think that I didn't realise this. Around this time, Chief Superintendent Ned Ryan came back to visit me. He was with my mother around 12.00 pm when I returned home. He repeated verbatim the original warning he gave me about the Provisional IRA mole within the Special Detective Unit. I think he came back to repeat the warning as senior Garda Officers had assessed the threat against me as extremely high.

At the end of July, two detectives, who were not doing security, entered the shop and introduced themselves as Detective Garda Sargent Austin Canavan and Detective Sargent Patrick Brennan, both of whom were from the Central Detective Unit. They wanted to interview me, and we made arrangements for the interview to start in mid-August. At the commencement of the first interview, they stated the view of the Garda. The view of the Garda was that they had no interest in any member of Kelly's staff other than what cooperation they could obtain. As a consequence of this, I was not cautioned, and I did not bring a solicitor along with me. The tone of the interview was relaxed and friendly. Austin Canavan did the writing, and Patrick Brennan asked the questions. However, the mood changed in the middle of the interview when I brought up the payment made by Matthew Kelly to Haughey in the Royal Oak Pub in Finglas in 1981. Mr Haughey was the outgoing Taoiseach, and an election was called with the 1981 hunger strikes in the background. The purpose of the payment was to secure Mr Haughey's influence and support in getting the £2 million tax bill reduced to a level suitable for the Kelly family. After this evidence, the detectives became uneasy, and the tone of the remainder of the interview became tense. Normally, in police interviews, the interviewee is under pressure, but my statements on Haughey turned the tables on the interviewers, who became unsettled.

The interview lasted a month until the middle of September. We did not meet up every day because of my work commitments. One day, while there was no interview, Eamon Kelly appeared in Harcourt Square, visiting one of the offices in order to get a document signed. Dublin Metropolitan District Garda offices came to a standstill as staff rushed to the windows for a look at Ireland's number one criminal, who paraded around the square without a bother in the world. The following day, I returned to the interview and was told about Eamon Kelly's visit.

The two detectives then told me that Eamonn Kelly was the prime suspect behind seven murders, two of which I knew about.

In late September, I returned to Harcourt Square to sign the statement. The statement had to be typed up, and that took a few days. I entered the interview room, and the two detectives stood behind a desk. On the desk were two documents opened about halfway through. The document on the left was the manuscript written by Austin Canavan; the document on the right was the typed version of Austin Canavan's manuscript. Both documents were open on the same page. This page contained the paragraphs about the payment to Haughey. The two detectives demanded that I remove the two paragraphs from each statement. I refused, and all hell broke loose. After ten minutes, they realised that they were getting nowhere with me. They then asked me if I would sign the statements, and I said I would after I read both the statements. I then proceeded to read both statements, and when I was satisfied that each was in accordance with the other, I then signed the statements. The detectives then looked at each other, and a smile broke out on their faces. They then explained that they had just taken the longest statement, in a criminal investigation, in the history of the Garda, going back sixty-one years since its foundation.

For the record, the typed-up version of the manuscript reached fifty-two pages. I think that it is entirely appropriate that the Irish State's first-ever witness protection programme should produce the longest statement taken by the force in an investigation. The statement was historical because I had made allegations of Haughey receiving a payment in return for a favour requested, which is a bribe. I had just blown the whistle on Haughey receiving payments, which were the subject of two tribunals of enquiry, which took place years later and cost the taxpayer £IR90 million. I also linked Haughey to organised crime. Despite my allegations, Haughey was allowed to carry on as if nothing had happened. The only thing my evidence achieved was to instigate a cover-up. As Fine Gael was in power at the time, I left the interview room with the impression that Charles Haughey was the leader of Fine Gael.

Supporters of Haughey defended him to the hilt when people questioned his wealth. The general public struggled to reconcile the cost of his mansion with the Taoiseach's salary. Such people were branded as envious because they didn't have Haughey's knowledge of finance or his investment skills. Haughey was presented as an Irish equivalent of the American investor, Warren Buffett. A subsequent public inquiry, known as the *Moriarty Tribunal*, tore this myth to shreds. The work of the Moriarty Tribunal found that payments and benefits of €9 million were made by the country's leading businessmen to Haughey in order to maintain him in a lifestyle that he was not able to afford. All the business leaders said that they supported Haughey as they believed that he would create the right environment for their businesses to flourish. Not one of them said that they requested a favour. The Moriarty Tribunal opened in 1997.

Detective Garda Harry Murphy of the Special Task Force acted as a de facto shop steward for the hundred or so detective guards in the

Special Task Force. He was told that the Special Task Force was providing the security for the State's first witness protection programme. This was a contentious issue for the guards as the Special Task Force was set up to counter subversive activity and not to deal with organised crime. Detective Garda Harry Murphy told me that as this was the State's first witness protection programme, the Director of Public Prosecutions, Mr Eamonn Barnes, had taken control of the case in person. He had my statement on his desk, which contained the allegation of a payment by Matthew Kelly to Charles Haughey, for which Kelly sought the favour of having the Carpetdrome tax bill reduced to half the original demand. The DPP obviously decided to do nothing about this.

My statement established a link between Mr Charles Haughey—the former Taoiseach, the current leader of the opposition, and future Taoiseach—and organised crime. One of the beneficiaries of the payment was to be Eamonn Kelly, the country's number one criminal and a mass murderer. Mr Hughey allowed himself to be bribed by people who, for a period of two and a half years, were seriously planning the murder of members of the Garda Siochana and me. One evening at the beginning of October 1983, I went into the Glenside Public House on the way home from work. The bar was a circular-shaped one in which one could see all around the premises. The two detectives and I were ordering some drinks when a man approached the bar from the opposite end. I recognised him as Vinnie Doyle, the editor of the Evening Herald. He came up to the bar to have a closer look at us. He didn't realise that I had recognised him. The guards and I were regular visitors to this pub, so the locals were quite familiar with the setup. The newspaper editor gave me a very puzzled look. I have no doubt that my statement had upset the political establishment and that the government had put a hold on the files that the newspaper had on the Kelly Carpets' case. In other words, the files were only available to certain people. He didn't know the reason for this sanction, and he was puzzled as I didn't look like the type of person who would upset the government. If he had come over to me and introduced himself, I would have been delighted to explain to him what was going on.

On the afternoon of 19th October 1983, one of the detectives came in to warn me that he had just received a message that Matthew Kelly and Michael Deighan had been released from prison. There was a sense of urgency as Mountjoy Prison was only down the road from the shop. On the way home in the car, I turned on the radio to listen to the news. On one of the bulletins, it was announced that Matthew Kelly and Michael Deighan had been released by the Supreme Court and had their criminal contempt of court convictions quashed following a successful appeal. As the complainant, I was never informed about the hearing. I found out about the decision almost like every member of the public did, except that a guard told me. The following two paragraphs contain the Supreme Court judgement. As you can see, my name is mentioned in high places:

"This Court is satisfied that in cases of contempt in the face of the Court a High Court Judge has jurisdiction to deal with the matter summarily and to impose punishment where it is necessary to do so to protect the administration of justice.

Assuming for the purpose of this appeal that the allegations made in the present case would, if proved, amount to contempt in the face of the court, this court is of opinion that, having regard to the sequence in which witnesses gave their evidence and adverting in particular to the fact Mr McGoldrick had completed his evidence in the Companies Act matter, the necessity for the judge to hear and determine the contempt issue did not exist. In these circumstances these appeals will be allowed. The court will make an order for the release of the appellants."

I heard down the grapevine that after this hearing, when Mr Richard Cooke returned to his desk in the law library, he threw his wig on his desk in anger and then said to a colleague that the Kelly Case had gone political. A couple of weeks later, Mr Tuite arrived at the curtain shop with a colleague. He had an affidavit typed up and ready for me to sign. The purpose of the affidavit was to support a prosecution against Michael Deighan for perjury. A commissioner for oaths was waiting in a nearby solicitor's office, ready to have the affidavit sworn.

Back in July 1983, when I attended Mr Tuite's office, he interviewed me and took a statement from me. My statement contained an account of a meeting with Michael Deighan back in 1981. Deighan had confronted me with a letter he had received from Mr Tuite, requesting him to make income tax returns for six years. Income tax returns were enclosed with the letter sent by Mr Tuite. These forms were not attached to the letter that Michael Deighan showed me. Deighan accused me of dropping his name when I visited Mr Tuite's offices after the seizure of Carpetdrome books. He wanted to know how Mr Tuite had found out about him. I stood my ground and said that I had never mentioned his name to Mr Tuite. The meeting then ended. However, there was a certain amount of truth to what Deighan said. Eamonn Kelly told me to make out a cheque to Michael Deighan for several hundred pounds. I was to enter it in the books as rent paid for storing furniture in the premises on Deighan's farm in St Margaret's. Deighan never made the returns and was subsequently prosecuted for failure to make income tax returns. He swore under oath in the circuit court that he never received the letter requesting income tax returns for six years. It was an open and shut case of perjury, and there were shades of Al Capone in it.

In May 1984, Mr Byrne invited me to a meeting at Cooper & Lybrand's offices in Fitzwilton Place at 1.00 pm on a weekday. I took it that he wanted to obtain my consent to give evidence in the forthcoming case against Gaynor & Tuffy. Upon arrival at the reception, I was greeted by a member of staff who said that I was not entitled to say what I felt like in court. This was an obvious reference to a threat to name Mr. Haughey in the liquidator's forthcoming case against Gaynor & Tuffy. The source of this threat must have been my allegations against Mr Haughey made to the Garda in 1983. I don't know how a member of Coopers & Lybrand staff, whose identity I did not know and whom I had never met before, could tell me that I could not say what I liked in court. I felt that I was entitled to mention the Haughey payment because it was relevant to the case, and because it was in the public interest, and also because it was fundamental to the Kellys' tax strategy.

I expected a working lunch. In attendance at the meeting were Liquidator Patrick Byrne; his assistant, Ernest Burden; and solicitors,

Frank Sowman and Michael Wolfe from William Fry & Co. Immediately, a trolley of sandwiches, buns, and soft drinks was brought in. It being lunch time and me being hungry, I got stuck in. The problem was that nobody else started to eat. They basically wanted me to eat, while the other four refrained from eating and drinking. This was a strategy to stop me from talking. It became an embarrassment, so I stopped eating. Because I stopped eating, a large cigar was produced. It was the largest cigar I had ever smoked, and again, it was introduced to shut me up.

What was said at the meeting was all small talk. At no time was the forthcoming case against Gaynor & Tuffy discussed in detail. There was no mention of the transfer of stock from Carpetdrome to Carpetdrive-In, no mention of the circumstances leading up to the appointment of the first liquidator, Niall Harding, and the role of Gaynor & Tuffy in his appointment, and no mention of any meetings between me and Gaynor & Tuffy between March 1981 and May 1981 in connection with the liquidation. They did not have a copy of the statement that I gave to Mr Tuite.

I asked Byrne why he was taking the case against fellow chartered accountants, and he replied that standards in the profession needed to be upheld. He then started to complain about having to make a living out of the criminal fraternity. He then said that the case against Gaynor & Tuffy would be very tough. Of course, it would be very tough as nobody from Coopers & Lybrand or from William Fry & Co. was making any effort to prepare for the case with me. I was the principal witness for the liquidator, and without me, Byrne had no case. Byrne then asked me to attend a meeting with his counsel the following week, which I agreed to. So, the only positive thing that came out of the meeting was my consent to give evidence in favour of the liquidator.

With that, the meeting broke up. Byrne escorted me out, and in the corridor outside, he asked me if all this was about Haughey. To me, this was an obvious reference to the statement that I had given to the Gardai in 1983. That statement was given to the Gardai and to nobody else, so much for Garda confidentiality. Also, I didn't mention the Haughey payment in the statement that I gave to Mr Tuite of the Revenue Commissioners. Byrne then explained to me that he had defeated Charles Haughey in his third attempt to gain election to the Dáil in 1956. This was a bye-election caused by the death of Byrne's father, Alfred. Alfred Byrne was a highly respected politician due to his favourable treatment of the poor.

I knew that Patrick Byrne was the son of a very famous Irish politician and former Lord Mayor of Dublin. What I did not know was that the liquidator was a member of Dáil Éireann himself. Paddy Byrne stood as an Independent in the 1956 election. The other political parties decided not to run candidates out of respect for the late Alfred Byrne, except Fianna Fáil, who was represented by Charles Haughey. So, the election was a head-to-head contest between Byrne and Haughey, with Byrne winning by 17,000 votes to 12,000. So, Charles Haughey had been defeated at his third attempt to become a TD. Haughey was also unsuccessful in the previous two general elections in 1951 and 1954.

However, Haughey was successful in his fourth attempt in the 1957 general election. Haughey congratulated Byrne on his victory, and Haughey said that he only contested the election as a protest against the Inter-Party Coalition Government. Paddy Byrne was also re-elected in the 1957 general election, this time as a Fine Gael TD. He then told me that Ray McSharry, the minister for finance, was in touch with him twice. I doubt if McSharry contacted Byrne to discuss the weather; rather, he was following up on Matt Kelly's payment to Haughey to see if Byrne could do anything about the tax bill. This approach to Byrne obviously took place back in 1982 on a Friday before the commencement of the first High Court case, when frantic efforts were made to settle the case. However, these efforts were unsuccessful as either the liquidator or the Revenue, or both, refused to accept an offer from the Kellys to settle the case before it went to court. So, Paddy Byrne, liquidator and a former TD, was intrigued that he and Haughey had crossed paths again.

A week later, I arrived back in Fitzwilton Place for the meeting with Mr Byrne's counsel as previously arranged. Mr Richard Cooke SC and Mr Peter Kelly BL attended the meeting. Mr John Cooke SC did not attend the meeting. The atmosphere was tense, and we did not shake hands. Mr Peter Kelly attacked me over the transfer of stock from Carpetdrome to Carpetdrive-In, accusing me of committing fraud. If he felt that way about it, I could not understand why they were still going ahead with the case against Gaynor & Tuffy. Mr Peter Kelly started to talk about his experience with Michael Deighan. Mr Peter Kelly was a junior counsel for the Sunday World in the action for defamation taken by Michael Deighan against the newspaper. He went on to tell me that his car was broken into in Clontarf, and his documents dealing with the Sunday World case were stolen, putting the blame on Deighan. This, at least, gave him something to talk about and to pass the time while avoiding the real issues. At least, he showed empathy with my current circumstances.

Going back to the High Court hearing on Monday, 27th June 1983, when I was in the witness box, I was sitting just a couple of feet in front of Mr Richard Cooke SC. Mr Justice Costello was busy organising the arrest of Kelly and Deighan. Cooke caught my attention, and as we looked at each other, he kept nodding in the direction of Judge Costello. I turned in the direction of Judge Costello and nodded back at Cooke, acknowledging that I understood that Cooke was encouraging me to give it everything, as I was in a unique position—having the ear of a High Court judge who wielded enormous power. As Cooke's house had been firebombed a year earlier, he had my empathy, so I gave it my best shot.

However, one year later, Mr Richard Cooke's attitude had completely changed towards me. He was showing no appetite for the forthcoming case either, because the case was a lost cause, having gone political, or because he and his team of barristers were in effect State employees who represented the Revenue Commissioners, and they were told by the government to lay off. Looking back at this meeting years later, I feel that Mr Richard Cooke SC was annoyed with me for depriving him of justice following the firebombing of his house. The

Supreme Court had quashed the conviction of Michael Deighan and Matthew Kelly for criminal contempt of court and had ordered their early release. The forthcoming case against Gaynor & Tuffy was not being properly prepared by the appellant and his legal representatives, and eventually, no further cases were taken against the Kelly brothers.

Mr Richard Cooke then started to talk about old Dublin cake shops. This was ironic, considering the display of cakes and buns presented at the previous week's meeting with the intention of distracting me from talking about the case. At no stage did we discuss the case against Gaynor & Tuffy. This was in complete contrast to the High Court hearing in 1983, when Richard Cooke was encouraging me to give it everything when giving my evidence. They did not have a copy of the statement that I gave to Mr Tuite. I expected them to have a copy of this statement so that they might ask me to elaborate on points that I had made in the statement. They never discussed meetings I had with Fergal Gaynor, nor did they ask me any questions about the events leading up to the liquidation of Carpetdrome. They made no effort to prepare for the forthcoming trial, such as discussing my evidence with me. Even though they had no case without me, they were treating me as a hostile witness.

All this affected my performance as a witness. Richard Cooke SC, I have no doubt, had come to the conclusion that the case was a lost cause, because the allegation that I had made against Mr Haughey had upset the Irish government. Coopers & Lybrand were preparing a political show trial in their offices. The objective of the show trial was to lose the case and, therefore, to discredit me. They were deliberately going out of their way to lose a case that was winnable, at huge expense to the Irish Taxpayer, in order to scapegoat me. The political show trial was being organised by Patrick Byrne, an accountant, a liquidator, and a former TD, in order to protect another TD who was also Taoiseach. I don't think one could stoop much lower in this life than scapegoating a witness when that witness was risking his life to give evidence in court cases. Coopers & Lybrand were appointed in the High Court as liquidators of Carpetdrome on the petition of the Revenue Commissioners, and as such, they became agents of the State. The expenses of the liquidation were guaranteed in the event that they recovered no money from the Kellys. Years later, they changed their name to *Price Waterhouse Coopers*. May I suggest that a more appropriate name would have been *Price Watergate Coopers!*

The liquidators' action against Gaynor & Tuffy opened in the High Court on Monday, 28th May 1984. The hearing was before Mr Justice O'Hanlon, who had replaced Mr Justice Costello, who had stepped down as he had passed judgement on my evidence in the 1983 hearing, which was now about to be challenged again, this time professionally. This was the third consecutive case in three years taken by the liquidator of Carpetdrome. It was also the final trial before the courts in connection with the affairs of Carpetdrome. The hearing took place on the top floor of the Four Courts in a small chamber, which was the furthest one away from the entrance to the Four Courts. I have no doubt that this courtroom was selected in order to make it difficult for members of the public to find, and also to tone down public interest in the case. The usual attendees showed up, such as the liquidator and his assistant, and Mr Tuite and his Revenue staff. What I noticed was the absence of the regular court reporters who were present at the previous two trials and whom I was familiar with. Also, no photographers were in attendance. Somebody in the courtroom was reporting to the press and acting as a censor, and I have no doubt that if I had mentioned the payment to Haughey, it would not have been reported in the newspapers. The respondents had engaged Mr Colm Condon SC, Mr Brian McCracken SC, and Mr James Salafia BL to represent them, and they were instructed by George D Fottrell Solicitors.

Mr Colm Condon SC was a former attorney general who organised the prosecution for the State against Haughey and others, in the *Arms Trial* of 1970. His reputation was awesome. He had attended Terenure College while I had gone to St Mary's College, Rathmines. Those who are familiar with these two schools will be aware of the intense rivalry between the two colleges, particularly on the rugby pitch. Now, it was Terenure versus Mary's in the High Court. Mr Condon SC was assisted by Mr Brian McCracken SC. Mr McCracken went on to chair a tribunal of inquiry in 1997 into payments made by Ben Dunne Junior to Charles Haughey, Michael Lowry, and others. I find it an extraordinary coincidence that the plaintiff, Mr Byrne, who had defeated Mr Haughey in the 1956 Dublin North East by-election in a head to head contest, Mr Condon, who had organised the prosecution against Mr Haughey in the Arms Trial, and Mr McCracken, who would head a future tribunal of enquiry into payments made to Mr Haughey, had such significant roles in this court case while an allegation of a payment to Mr Haughey by Matt Kelly lurked in the background.

This was the liquidators' case against Gaynor & Tuffy:

"They crucially assisted the winding down of Carpetdrome in a particular manner that enabled the substance of that business to be separated from Carpetdrome and reestablished as Carpetdrive-In, carrying on the same business in the same premises with the same stock and divesting itself of creditors. The whole significance of this case was not that some creditors were paid but that quite deliberately a whole class or group of creditors were assured they would be paid in full and were in fact paid in full – creditors who were vital to continuing the carpet trade – so that they would continue to support the new business in its new manifestation. The respondents were fully and knowingly involved in all the ramifications of the transfer of the Carpetdrome business into Carpetdrive-In."

Mr Justice O'Hanlon had never looked so comfortable to me during the trial. I have no doubt that he was interfered with due to my Garda statement, which implicated Haughey. I have no doubt that had I mentioned the payment to Haughey, he would have collapsed the case there and then on a technicality. So, on Wednesday afternoon, 30th May 1984, I entered the witness box to start my direct evidence. Mr Richard Cooke SC started the examination.

To me, the case centred around a series of meetings that I had with Mr Gaynor at his offices, where we discussed the transfer of stock between Carpetdrome and Carpetdrive-In around April 1981. Mr Gaynor later denied that any of these meetings took place in his evidence to the court. The judge dismissed these meetings, in his judgement, because I did not have accurate dates. So, I then started to discuss the transfer between Carpetdrome and Carpetdrive-In when Judge O'Hanlon made an interruption to warn me that I was not obliged to incriminate myself. This obviously threw me off, and I aborted a large part of my evidence. I should have replied to the judge that the Garda view was that they had no interest in any member of staff other than what cooperation they could obtain. This, in effect, ruled out the possibility of any prosecution against me. Unfortunately, I did not think of this at the time. The rest of the evidence I have mentioned in the chapters leading up to this, so there is no point in repeating it.

Mr Condon SC then commenced his cross-examination. His first point was that I had withheld information about the second set of sales books from Mr Gaynor's employee, Mr Tom Cullen, when Mr Cullen asked me about the difficulty the Carpetdrome had in paying its bills. My answer to that was that when Mr Gaynor called to introduce Mr Cullen to me and to advise me that he would be working two days a week on a part-time basis, I told Mr Gaynor that there was a bit of a fiddle going on here. His reply was that I was never to discuss the affairs of Carpetdrome with anybody. I take it that that included Mr Cullen. I then told Mr Gaynor about Roundwood Carpets in the UK and that he would have to look at their accounts in conjunction with Carpetdrome accounts, to which I got no response. Mr Gaynor, in court, denied that these conversations ever took place.

Eamon Kelly was running a reign of terror from the Phibsborough store, and for Mr Cullen's safety, I didn't mention the existence of a second set of books, which were known as the *'Hookey Books'* or *'Eamons Books'* when Mr Cullen asked me about Carpetdrome's difficulty in paying its bills. My fears about Mr Cullen's safety were justified when his car was broken into, and his working papers were stolen in November 1980. The purpose of the break-in to his car was to secure an adjournment of a tax appeal concerning Matt Kelly's tax affairs. Unfortunately, I did not think of mentioning my fears for Mr Cullen's safety in my reply to Mr Condon.

His second point was that there was a scheme to fund the transfer from Carpetdrome to Carpetdrive-In. I denied that such a scheme existed, and I was surprised at his suggestion. He then asked about the €8,000 loan account in my name. I replied that this was not my money. I did not handle this point very well. I should have explained that four sums of money arrived in Carpetdrive-In bank's current account at the end of June 1981, which I could not reconcile with sales. I allocated three of the sums to the three directors, Paul Jackson, Eamonn Kelly, and Thomas Kelly. This left the fourth and smallest sum at a loose end, so I put it in my name. This was a stupid mistake on my behalf, and a couple of weeks later, I took the sum out of my name and put it into a suspense account. These transactions later turned out to be excessive unrecorded sales, which had to be recycled in order to pay creditors and had nothing to do with the transfer from Carpetdrome to Carpetdrive-In. Eamon Kelly told me to put these amounts down as *directors' loans*. It was company policy that any transaction that needed an explanation was described as a loan of some sort. The Carpetdrive-In was trading fraudulently, just like its predecessor, the Carpetdrome.

Mr Gaynor later said in court that I told him, at the time of the transfer, that I was putting money into the Carpetdrive-In. I never said this because, at that time, I had very little money left after buying a motor car, and I had only been working for two years at the most. After I left the witness box, I complained bitterly to Mr Byrne about Mr Richard Cooke's performance, to which I got the reply that Dick had gone past his best, an obvious reference to Mr Cooke's age, as he was in his early seventies. Mr John Cooke SC then proceeded to read out a list of UK cases as precedents, mentioning the key point of the judgement in each case. The judge thanked him for his contributions. However, I feel that Mr John Cooke SC would have rendered a better service if he had concentrated on the case that he and his father were presenting, rather than quoting precedents.

On Tuesday, 5th June, Mr McCracken made an application to the court to have the case dismissed on the grounds that Gaynor & Tuffy did not have a case to answer, and Mr Justice O'Hanlon reserved judgement, which caused an adjournment of the case. About a week later, the court reconvened. The judge said that Gaynor & Tuffy had a case to answer. He said that, even though he considered me to be a party to the fraud, he could not dismiss my allegations out of hand. I was surprised that he had not dismissed the case for two reasons. The first reason was that he had blocked my evidence on the transfer between

Carpetdrome and Carpetdrive-In when he warned me about self-incrimination. The second reason was that the liquidators' lawyers had treated me as if I were a hostile witness and went out of their way to lose the case through inadequate preparation at a meeting with me and an under examination of me in the witness box.

As I have said earlier, I have no doubt that the judge was interfered with, and when I did not mention the payment to Haughey, he then felt that the interference was unjustified. He then moved to assert his independence and that of his fellow judges by finding that Gaynor & Tuffy had a case to answer. Mr Colm Condon SC then rose to his feet in a state of panic. He had booked a flight to the USA for a business trip over the weekend, and so the case had to be adjourned for about two weeks until he returned.

A very flustered Mr Condon pulled out his diary to confirm dates with the judge. As there was no internet back in those days, a trip to the USA was not something done at the drop of a hat. His arrangements to go to the United States must have been made well in advance of the trial. These arrangements were made in expectation of the judge making a determination that the accountants did not have a case to answer. What there was no doubt about was that the former attorney general of Ireland was in contempt of court. His offence was similar to a witness who, while under subpoena, failed to show up for a hearing. He should have been punished accordingly, just like the rest of us. Mr Condon had booked a trip to the USA before the completion of a full hearing, and Condon thought that the case would end after the respondent applied for a non-suit. The fact that he forecast incorrectly a non-suit shows breathtaking arrogance on his part. It is the decision of the presiding judge to determine if Gaynor & Tuffy had a case to answer, not Mr Condon's.

One afternoon, just before 2 pm, when we were waiting for the court to reconvene, I overheard Mr Richard Cooke and Mr Condon having a conversation. Cooke asked Condon why he hadn't become a judge, and Condon replied that he would only become a judge if the government would make him the chief justice. This meant that he would not be serving beforehand as a judge of the High Court or the Supreme Court. No government would appoint a barrister straight to the chief justice, as it would be too controversial.

As I left the court, I noticed that Fergal Gaynor and Patrick Tuffy were shattered and were being comforted by their lawyers. A finding by a High Court judge that they had a case to answer in the performance of their professional duties was what they had tried to avoid. If the judge had found that they had no case to answer, that would have been the end of the matter, and there would never be any mention of the case again. However, as he found out that they had a case to answer, his judgement in the matter of Kelly's Carpetdrome Limited (in liquidation) and in the matter of the Companies Act 1963 and Gaynor & Tuffy became one of lasting significance. This judgement will be available in perpetuity to law students and practitioners and will also appear in legal textbooks. So, when Mr Condon SC returned from America, the trial resumed with the hearing of the defence's case.

On 13th July 1984, Mr Justice O'Hanlon returned his judgement. Fergal Gaynor and Patrick Tuffy were exonerated and cleared. Costs were apportioned as two-thirds to the liquidator and one-third to Gaynor & Tuffy. He made an adverse finding against me. He found that I was a party to the fraud. As I was not a party to the proceedings, I had no representation. I was neither appellant nor respondent; I was just a witness. As well as not being represented, the liquidator's lawyers were trying to lose the case, which affected my performance in court. I have no doubt that I had suffered an injustice.

CHAPTER 6

NOLLE PROSEQUI

"The only thing necessary for the triumph of evil is for good men to do nothing."
—Edmund Burke

On a Sunday morning in August 1983, I turned on the *BBC* to watch their news bulletin. The main item on the bulletin was the attempted kidnapping of the Canadian billionaire retailer, Galen Weston. A Provisional IRA gang was intercepted on his estate in Roundwood County, Wicklow. A gun battle then ensued between the Garda Special Task Force and the Provisional IRA. Several of the Provisional IRA team were injured in the shoot-out. There were no fatalities. None of the Gardai were injured. The BBC report showed a group of Special Task Force officers assembled outside the estate's gate lodge. I recognised everyone in that group. I was on first-name terms with all of them, as they had been doing security on me since the end of June. It was at this point that the gravity of my predicament really sank in.

In November 1983, Don Tidey, an Englishman and a supermarket executive, was kidnapped near his home in Rathfarnham. He was then taken to Ballinamore in County Leitrim. The Garda Special Task Force led the search for Tidey and were backed up by the army and Garda recruits from Templemore. However, the full complement of Garda Special Task Force officers could not be deployed because they had to retain officers back in Dublin in order to protect me. It took eight armed officers a day to provide protection for me. While searching for Tidey in the woods near Ballinamore, the Garda Special Task Force encountered the Provisional IRA again. This time, one of their members was shot. Detective Garda Donnie Kelleher was shot in the legs and was hospitalised. Subsequently, due to his injuries, he was withdrawn from the Garda Special Task Force. Due to the efforts of the Garda Special Task Force and the Irish Army, Don Tidey was recaptured and set free. Trainee Garda Gary Sheehan and Army Private Patrick Kelly were killed in the shoot-out.

When Don Tidey returned home, he was placed under Garda protection. Rathfarnham Garda Station was put under enormous pressure trying to provide security for former Taoiseach, Liam Cosgrave, Don Tidey, and me, as we all lived in Rathfarnham. Reinforcements were brought in from Tallaght Garda Station to help out.

In March 1984, the Garda Special Task Force approached a house in Newmarket-on-Fergus in County Clare. Dominic McGlinchey was in an upstairs bedroom in the house and opened fire on the Garda car. A ferocious gun battle ensued, and the Special Task Force car was riddled with bullets while the detectives took shelter behind the car. Detective

Garda Christy Power was shot in the shoulder and had to wait until McGlinchey surrendered before he was taken away for treatment. Due to his injuries, Detective Garda Christy Power was withdrawn from the Special Task Force.

On the way home one evening, I went through the traffic lights as they turned red. This meant that the Garda escort car had to stop and wait for the lights to turn green. When the Garda car caught up with me, I got an earful from Detective Garda Frank Hayes. He explained to me that recently, a motorcycle with a pillion passenger was spotted by the detectives following behind me, acting suspiciously. The motorcycle was manoeuvring between the Garda car and my car and pulled up alongside my car. When the guards checked out the motorcycle's number, the plates turned out to be false. There is no doubt that the pair on the motorcycle was simulating an assassination attempt.

After the 1984 High Court case, the Garda protection continued on as normal as it was on the first day. Around this time, a senior Garda officer met up with George Allis privately. The officer told George that, despite the protection, the guards could not guarantee my safety. Garda intelligence, which is obviously collected from informers, had indicated that an attack on me and those protecting me was expected. The officer wanted to know from George if he should tell me about this threat. George strongly advised him not to tell me, and the officer didn't. After the protection was withdrawn, George told me about this meeting. He also told me that the guards had increased the security, unknown to me at the time, by placing two extra cars in the vicinity of the shop: one in

Phibsborough shopping centre and the other on St Peter's Road behind Dalymount Park. Each extra car contained two heavily armed members of the Special Task Force. Without a doubt, I was the highest-protected person in the country. These arrangements went on for a considerable period of time.

On a lighter note, I attended the Rugby International between Ireland and Wales on Saturday, 4th February 1984. This was the day that the new East Stand was opened. The guards had all the passes necessary to get themselves and their car into the ground. I travelled to the ground in the Garda car for convenience. There were two car parks beside the ground with access from a lane off Shelbourne Road. The one on the left was the larger of the two. The one on the right, which was right behind the West Stand, only held about six cars. The Garda passes entitled us to enter the smaller car park. The Taoiseach's car was already parked there; it really was the Holy of Holies!

One of the detectives opened the briefcase on the bonnet of the car, exposing the five magazines already in the case, while the other detective decommissioned the Uzi submachine gun by removing its magazine and placing the two items in their respective slots in the case. There were a large number of stewards present, and there were gasps of disbelief at what they were watching. There was a uniformed Garda sergeant on duty, and one of the stewards asked him what was going on. "The Kelly Case," was the swift reply that I overheard. The chief steward then came over to me and asked if I had a ticket. I put my hand in my pocket and produced a humble terrace ticket. The chief steward then examined the ticket and said, "That's fine," and asked me to follow him. He then escorted us around to the other side of the ground to the new East Stand and to the correct point of entry. I thanked him for his assistance.

I had a standing arrangement with the guards to play golf in nearby Stackstown Golf Club, which was owned by the guards. Two detectives, who were interested in golf, were selected for duty and had brought their golf clubs with them on the Sunday morning.

One Sunday morning, we arrived just before a hastily arranged golf competition was about to start. We were given very little time to change. We rushed out to the first tee and drove off. The first fairway ran parallel to the clubhouse, with the bar upstairs overlooking the fairway. I heard fierce banging on the bar window and looked up at a man trying to catch our attention. He was pointing back towards the tee box. I then saw that he was pointing at a magnum .38 hand gun, which a detective had dropped in haste. So, one of the detectives ran back and retrieved the gun.

On another occasion, in the summer of 1984, we went up to Pine Valley Par 3 golf course on a weekday evening. The detectives hired golf clubs, which were contained in a pencil-type bag. As there was no room in the bags to hold their guns, we put all the guns in my golf bag, which was a large tournament-type bag. When we reached the second tee, there was a queue to tee off as the second hole was a difficult hole, and it was a blustery evening. An elderly gentleman in front of us teed off and hit a very poor shot. In actual fact, you could throw the ball further. In embarrassment, he turned around to the gallery and proclaimed that what he needed was a machine gun to fire the golf ball. Well, my hand went for the zip on my golf bag. I held back and didn't offer him the machine gun. I guessed that this would have triggered a Garda enquiry and probably gotten the two detectives into trouble. Anyway, if I had produced the machine gun and offered it to him, I think the shock would have killed him.

That same summer, I left the house on a weekday morning with the Garda escort. I drove to the top of the road where there was a junction, and I stopped. So, I looked right up Orwell Road towards Mount Carmel Hospital. Mount Carmel Hospital was situated at the top of a hill. I noticed two cars coming down the hill in close proximity to each other. As the cars came closer to me, I could see that the front car was chauffeur-driven with a bald-headed passenger in the back. Behind the front car was a Garda Special Branch car with two plainclothes detectives in the front seats. It was the minister for justice, Michael Noonan, on his way into work under Garda escort. I then turned left onto Orwell Road, as I had intended to do, and caught up with Minister Noonan.

"Well," I said to myself, "fancy that!" You just couldn't make this up—Minister Noonan in his chauffeur-driven front car, followed by his Garda Special Branch escort, then followed by me, and finally my Garda Special Task Force escort. This was truly unique, so I did everything possible to keep the convoy of four cars together for as long as possible. So, I followed Minister Noonan through Rathgar and Rathmines and then to the government buildings on Merrion Row, where we parted company.

My sister, Helen, got married in the summer of 1984. I was the eldest of five siblings, and with my father deceased, I was expected to give her away. However, she wasn't happy about travelling to the church, followed by armed detectives. It sounded like the ultimate shotgun wedding. So, I stood back, and a man married to my father's sister deputised for me.

In November 1984, a customer came into the shop and ordered two small pairs of curtains for his sitting room. He needed the two pairs for a party on the following Saturday night. The customer lived in a mews off Palmerston Road. I said that I would be passing his mews on my way home and would drop the two pairs of curtains off for him. He told me that the mews was on a lane way off Palmerston Road, directly behind Garret Fitzgerald's house. As Garret Fitzgerald was Taoiseach, he had Garda security at his home. The customer then became very concerned about my safety. There was a hut in Garret Fitzgerald's front garden that sheltered the guards on duty. Palmerston Road was a busy road, so one had to be quick to get through the traffic and on to the lane where the mews was located. The customer was very concerned that the Garda in the hut would open fire on me if I was not careful enough. I assured him that there was no way that they would open fire on me!

Ireland beat England on 30th March 1985 to win the Triple Crown. This was obviously a cause for celebration. On the following day, I went out to Dublin Airport to see off a friend of mine, Kevin O'Connor, who had travelled over from the UK to attend the match. On the way back from the airport, I stopped in the Garda Club on Harrington Street to have a drink and to facilitate the changing of the guard. Sounds a bit like the Tower of London or Buckingham Palace! Harcourt Square, where the Special Task Force was based, was very close to Harrington Street. At 7.00 pm, the change of the guard took place. One of the two guards who came on duty was very drunk, and the other was a teetotaller. So, I decided to leave the Garda Club and head back home. I walked up the South Circular Road, followed by the Special Task Force car. However, the detective following me was struggling to walk and had to support himself by hanging out of the lamppost. After a minute or two hanging out of the lamppost, he made an effort to reach the next lamppost. He then steadied himself by wrapping his arms around the lamppost. This process was repeated until we reached Leonard's Corner, where I got on a bus on Clanbrassil Street, and the detective on foot got into the Garda car and followed the bus back to my home. Later, I learned from another detective that the drunk garda's sergeant was following in another car behind the car following me. So, we had a procession up the South Circular Road led by me, followed by the guard supported by the lampposts, followed by his colleague in the escort car, and then followed by their sergeant in another unmarked Garda car. This procession was a source of great amusement amongst members of the Garda Special Task Force.

In June 1985, my friend, Kevin O'Connor, returned from the UK for a holiday to visit friends and relatives. I joined up with him for a few days in Kerry. This was my first holiday in several years, as my holiday entitlements were used up attending court cases and interviews with the Revenue, the liquidator, and the guards, for which I got no thanks. We stayed in Ballybunion, and I played the course twice. Kevin arrived in Ireland with a white MG sports car fitted with a collapsible roof and carrying a UK registration plate. The sports car with the roof down, followed by a Garda escort driving up and down the main street of Ballybunion, attracted a lot of attention. Curiosity got the better of a local journalist who worked for *The Kerryman* newspaper. The journalist approached the guards to find out what was going on. The response he got was that the guards were minding a cousin of the queen!

In the Autumn of 1985, the guards asked me if I could help out with their rugby side, which was doing quite well. They wanted me to take up training with the Garda Rugby Club on a Tuesday and a Thursday evening each week in order to facilitate members of the Special Task Force who were on the Garda Rugby side. I agreed to this, despite not having played rugby since I left school 10 years earlier. The class I was in at St Mary's College had Rodney O'Donnell (Leinster, Ireland, and British & Irish Lions test player), Declan Fanning (Leinster and Irish Final Trialist), and Declan Howard (Leinster). Rodney O'Donnell happened to be the pupil I sat beside on my first day in St Mary's back in 1963.

Despite being in such distinguished rugby company, I wasn't much use at the game. However, anybody who went to St Mary's College for the eleven years left with a great grounding in the skills of rugby. Those who were involved in the Garda Rugby Club were definitely not from the rugby heartlands of South Dublin, but rather from a GAA background. They were totally mesmerised by the bounce of the oval ball. One evening, I overheard them refer to me as *'the gouger.'* That was because, having worked for the Kellys, I surprised them with my handling and passing skills that took years to develop, skills that a gouger is not supposed to possess. I can see why the GAA classified Rugby Union Football as a foreign game.

January 1986 arrived, and the protection was now entering its fourth calendar year. In the first week of February, I got a call from two detectives at work. One of the detectives was Austin Canavan, who had interviewed me back in 1983. The other detective was Fachtna Murphy, who had recently joined the Fraud Squad. Fachtna Murphy later became the Garda Commissioner in 2007. The purpose of their visit was to inform me that the director of public prosecutions had made a decision not to take any prosecutions against the Kellys. I asked for an explanation, and I was told that the DPP never gave an explanation when he made a decision not to prosecute. You just had to accept it as it was. There was no mention of my affidavit alleging perjury against Michael Deighan, so I took it that all prosecutions were off. I am not sure if the two detectives from the Central Detective Unit were aware of the existence of the affidavit, as it was organised by Mr Tuite of the Revenue Commissioners.

Needless to say, I never heard any more about this affidavit from the Revenue Commissioners. I then asked what would happen to the security, and I was told that decisions on security were a matter for Garda headquarters only. There was no mention of relocation, a new identity, or a new passport. The meeting then broke up. The news came as a shock to me. I was told, when I signed the statement in 1983, that it would be a long investigation and that I would have to be patient. I wasn't prepared for this, and it felt like an anti-climax. I also never retracted my statement, and I never expressed any reservations about giving evidence against the Kellys if required to do so.

Two weeks later, I got a visit from Detective Sargent Jude Murphy, who told me that round-the-clock security would continue until mid-March. It would then be scaled back to one detective in the evenings and through the night for two weeks until the last Monday morning in March, when the protection would finish.

So, let's recap on what had just happened. Mr Justice Costello, a former attorney general, had referred the case to the director of public prosecutions to consider criminal charges against the Kelly brothers. Costello was the last attorney general to exercise the power of criminal prosecution because he created the office of director of public prosecutions and transferred the prosecuting powers of the attorney general to that office in 1973. Costello's successor, Eamon Barnes, had made a decision not to prosecute in the Kelly case, a case that was referred to him by the creator of his office.

CHAPTER 7

THE AFTERMATH

"Laws are like cobwebs, which may catch small flies, but let wasps and hornets break through."
—Johnathan Swift circa 1700.

Life returned to normal in April 1986 after the protection was withdrawn. In the beginning, it took time to get used to the protection, and in the end, it took time to get used to the fact that it was gone, as I had spent two years and nine months under round-the-clock protection. That summer, an unmarked Garda car, with three occupants, pulled up alongside me on the North Circular Road. The window came down, and a voice asked me how I was getting on and if I had any problems. I replied that I was getting on fine and that I had no problems. The response to the reply was a huge roar of laughter, and the window went back up, and the car sped off. I have no doubt that the guards had very strong words with members of the Kelly family when they delivered the decision of the DPP not to prosecute them.

Around this time, a VAT issue arose between the Revenue Commissioners and George Allis's trading company, G & C Curtains

Ltd. George had taken over the stock of fabrics from Carpetdrome when it ceased to trade. An invoice for the stock was issued by Carpetdrome that included IR€10,000 for VAT. George Allis and the supplier, Carpetdrome, were not connected parties and, therefore, his company was entitled to the VAT credit. The Revenue never refunded the VAT return, which included the IR€10,000 credit. The result of this was that he could not pay the VAT liability on the next six returns. The Revenue then sent the six unpaid VAT returns to the Sheriff for collection while ignoring the claim for a refund, in effect, refusing the offset. The accountant dealing with the case commented to me that he had never seen such an aggressive stance from both the sheriff and the Revenue. An appeal was lodged and listed for hearing, following a VAT inspection at the company's offices.

A couple of days before the hearing, I got a call from the accountant who told me that the case was being withdrawn by the Revenue, who had agreed to accept the refund due on the first VAT return. A small refund from the Revenue followed after offsetting the amounts on the VAT returns. If the disputed VAT credit had been disallowed, then George Allis's business would have folded up. I have no doubt that his business was targeted because he employed me. If his business had to close down in the middle of a recession, I would have found it impossible to get employment, as a former protected state witness had little or no appeal to any potential employer.

On Saturday, April 27th, 1987, the final of the Leinster Senior Rugby Cup took place at Lansdowne Road. The finalists were Lansdowne

Football Club and St Mary's Rugby Football Club. My old classmate, Declan Fanning, captained St Mary's on that beautiful spring afternoon. I watched the game from the terraces below the East Stand. I positioned myself at the 22-metre line. During the first half, there was an air of tension among the spectators, with a lot of people conversing with each other. I moved towards the halfway line, where the crowd was denser. I eavesdropped on the conversations. People were discussing an IRA bomb that went off at the border at lunchtime. It transpired that a judge and his wife had been killed in the explosion. The judge was Maurice Gibson, who was a judge of the appeal court in Northern Ireland, and his wife was Lady Cecily Gibson. I also established that three Irish rugby squad members, who were travelling in the opposite direction to Dublin for a training session, were also injured in the explosion. They were David Irwin, Philip Rainey, and Nigel Carr. Nigel Carr never played again due to his injuries. As I got a grip of the situation, a shiver ran down my spine as I realised that the IRA mole in the Special Detective Unit must have had a hand in this atrocity. So, this was the work of the mole that Chief Superintendent Ned Ryan had warned me about on two occasions back in 1983.

The judge and his wife arrived at Dun Laoghaire ferry port at 9.00 pm that morning. They were met by Detective Garda Noel Motson and another detective, who escorted them up to the border. Detective Garda Noel Motson provided protection for me on several occasions. When they reached the border, the two cars stopped, and the judge got out of his car to shake hands with the two detectives and to thank them for the escort. He got back into his own car and proceeded towards his RUC escort, which was about a hundred yards away. About halfway between the Garda car and the RUC car, a bomb went off, killing the judge and his wife instantly. The bomb was in a culvert on the side of the road and was triggered from a distance. The accuracy and timing of the bomb were such that it could only have been put together with information supplied by the Provisional IRA mole in Harcourt Square, who, through his position, had access to the Gibsons' security arrangements following their return to Ireland from their holidays abroad.

In the autumn of 1987, George Allis took a claim against Dublin Corporation for the malicious damage to his company's stock caused by the Carpetdrome fire. This followed a prompt from a barrister when George was measuring up for curtains in his house. I would be a key witness in the claim. In the Spring of 1988, I attended a meeting with Mr John Gordon SC as part of the preparation for the forthcoming case in the Four Courts. The meeting broke up at 4.00 pm, and as I was walking through the Round Hall, I encountered a barrister whom I knew, leaving one of the four courts off the Round Hall. It was my old classmate, Peter Charleton, who suggested that we go for a drink. He went off for a few minutes to disrobe himself, and when he came back, we went downstairs to a small bar in the basement of the Four Courts beside the coffee shop. He was pleased to see me as he had followed the Kelly Case closely. He did not have to rely on legal reports to follow the case, as there was wall-to-wall coverage of the case in the newspapers. So, naturally, we discussed the Kelly Case, which he was very interested in. He made two comments that have always stood out in my mind. The first was that the *Kelly Case had brought to the attention of the legal profession the rising threat of organised crime*. The second comment he made was that *if Judge Declan Costello had heard the Gaynor & Tuffy case, then there would have been an entirely different outcome*. After about an hour, we parted company.

Dublin Corporation engaged the services of the accountancy firm, Stokes Kennedy Crowley, to deal with the stock loss claim. I dealt with Noel Cooke, a partner in SKC. As George's company was only trading for about a full year at the time of the fire, there was no stocktaking done, and no stock records were available. This made negotiations with Noel Cooke very difficult, and so the case went to court. The case was listed for June 1988.

On the morning of the hearing, George Allis, Feilim O'Reilly, his solicitor, John Gordon, his barrister, and I all met up outside the circuit court. Negotiations then started with the barrister for Dublin Corporation. The barrister for Dublin Corporation was none other than Peter Kelly, now a senior counsel—what a coincidence! I spoke to Peter Kelly and recited my evidence about the fire. He had heard the same evidence in court years earlier when he represented the liquidator in the Kelly Case. The case was then settled, with an offer made to George Allis, which he accepted. I have no doubt that Peter Kelly was handpicked for this case because of his involvement in the Kelly Case and his previous dealings with me. He was also under instructions to settle the malicious damage claim, and under no circumstances was he to let the case go into the courtroom, thus preventing me from giving evidence and, perhaps, mentioning the Haughey payment.

In November 1984, an incident took place in the Workers' Party social club in Gardiner Place. A row broke out between Eamon Kelly and Patrick Querney, a Workers' Party activist in Ballymun. Querney had asked one of the Kelly gang to stop playing a slot machine. The following evening, Eamon Kelly returned to the club with a number of associates and waited inside the club for Querney to appear. When Querney arrived, he was stabbed three times, twice in the heart. Querney survived the attack due to quick medical intervention.

The organisational structure of Sinn Féin, the Workers' Party, referred to Sinn Féin as 'Group A',[2] and the Official IRA as 'Group B,' in order to avoid the legal implications of using the term *IRA*. Group B's alliance with the Kelly gang broke down irrevocably following the stabbing. Querney made a statement to the guards, naming his assailants, after he was visited in hospital by both Pronsias De Rossa and Sean Garland, who both encouraged him to make a statement. Querney named Eamon Kelly as the assailant, and Kelly was charged with grievous bodily harm, malicious wounding, and assault.

Eamon Kelly's trial took place in the Circuit Criminal Court in early June 1986. Eamon Kelly tried to claim that the victim and other eyewitnesses had mistaken him for his brother, Matthew. Eamon Kelly

---

[2] The Lost Revolution, Brian Hanley and Scott Millar, 2010, Penguin Ireland.

said he wasn't there when the assault took place. The jury saw through all of this and convicted him.

In a plea for leniency, Kelly's counsel said that the case was an isolated incident and that he and his brother, Matthew, had undergone a very traumatic experience when their successful carpet business went to the wall because of troubles with the Revenue Commissioners. All I can say to that is these troubles were self-inflicted. Sentencing Kelly to ten years' imprisonment, Judge Gerard Buchanan described the stabbing as a vicious assault and said that the evidence revealed a story of intimidation and fear that was abhorrent to the ordinary citizens of Dublin. The judge added that he had searched the evidence for matters in Kelly's favour and could find none.

A year later, the Court of Criminal Appeal quashed Kelly's conviction and ordered a retrial. The new trial heard that one of the prosecution's witnesses had been convicted of manslaughter and that he had changed his original statement. Eamon Kelly claimed that he could not have been in the club on the night in question because he was barred from the club in 1982. He claimed that his brother, Matthew, had fought Querney. Another gang member testified that it was he rather than Kelly who had carried out the stabbing. The charges of grievous bodily harm and malicious wounding were dropped against Kelly, and his sentence was downgraded to three years for assault.

On 3rd September 1992, Eamon Kelly picked up John Conlon at Dublin airport. They drove into Dublin city centre, followed by a surveillance team from the Central Detective Unit. The purpose of

Conlon's visit to Dublin was to organise shipments of cocaine to Eamon Kelly. The US government had cracked down on the Colombian drug cartels. So, the Colombians were looking at new markets, in particular, Europe. Conlon had sourced a kilo of cocaine from his Colombian contacts, and this was a trial run. Kelly and Conlon drove to Jury's hotel in Ballsbridge to meet Elizabeth Yamanoha, a Cuban woman, who had just arrived on a flight from Miami, where Conlon had recruited her to courier the drugs. The Cuban woman had concealed the drugs in the layers of her body fat, and she handed over the drugs to Conlon. Kelly and Conlon then left Jury's hotel and headed for the north inner city. Detectives intercepted Kelly and Conlon at the East Link Toll Bridge, where they seized the drugs and arrested the pair. This seizure of cocaine was the biggest seizure of drugs yet recorded in Ireland.

In May 1993, Eamon Kelly and Elizabeth Yamanoha were convicted of the possession of one kilo of cocaine with a street value of IR€500,000. Conlon wasn't tried because he absconded on bail. Kelly received a thirteen-year term of imprisonment. Kelly claimed that another Irish criminal based in the UK had asked him to pick up Conlon at Dublin Airport and that he had no knowledge of a drug deal. Kelly also accused Conlon of setting him up to be arrested. The prosecutor for the State was my old classmate, Mr Peter Charleton SC. It was an extraordinary coincidence that my old classmate was prosecuting my former employer, Eamon Kelly, in such a high-profile case. In 2003, Eamon Kelly was released from prison, having served his time for cocaine trafficking. However, in those ten years, the cocaine business had mushroomed into a billion-euro industry. Despite all that happened in his absence, Eamon Kelly adapted to the new order and quickly resumed his influential position.

Just as Kelly had mentored Gerard Hutch some twenty years earlier, he began the same process again with Marlo Hyland and Eamon Dunne, also known as the *'Don.'* Eamon Kelly struck up a relationship with Eamon Dunne, and they were seen regularly together in the pubs and parks around Raheny, near where Eamon Kelly lived in Killester. St Anne's Park in Raheny was a favourite meeting place as it placed them outside the range of Garda listening devices.

As Eamon Kelly was a major influencer in the underworld, a lot of senior underworld figures switched their allegiance to Eamon Dunne. However, Eamon Dunne developed into a mass murderer, and between 2005 and 2010, Dunne had organised or carried out seventeen murders. It was obvious that Eamon Kelly had lost control of the Don to such an extent that Dunne started threatening other senior underworld figures; his days were numbered. On Friday, 23rd April 2010, Dunne was attending a fortieth birthday celebration event in the Fassaugh pub in Cabra when, at around 9.30 pm, a car pulled up outside the pub, and three armed, masked men got out. One of the men remained outside, and the other two entered the bar, where they picked out Eamon Dunne and shot him dead.

Eamon Kelly became embroiled in a feud with the Real IRA, who were trying to extort money from him, but Kelly refused to pay up. The outcome of this was a failed attempt on Kelly's life in 2010 when an assassin's gun jammed. Kelly then chased the gunman on foot, forcing him to flee. Kelly refused to report the incident to the Gardai, saying that he would deal with the matter in his own way. Alan Ryan, the Real IRA gang leader, had become a thorn in the side of the underworld. He was eventually gunned down in the street in September 2012 by two gunmen. The Real IRA blamed Eamon Kelly for Alan Ryan's murder.

On Tuesday, 4th December 2012, Eamon Kelly was shot dead near his home in Killester. The front-page headline in the *Irish Independent* the following morning proclaimed Eamon Kelly as the number one criminal in the state. As Eamon Kelly had mentored Gerard Hutch, Eamon Dunne, and Marlo Hyland, he was the closest that we have had to the godfather in Ireland.

The eulogy at his funeral was given by Dessie O'Hare. O'Hare, who had confessed to 27 murders, also acted as the pallbearer. O'Hare was also responsible for the kidnapping of the dentist, John O'Grady, and the severing of his fingers. Eamon Kelly and Dessie O'Hare had become friends while serving terms of imprisonment in Portlaoise prison. Kelly was a close drinking buddy of O'Hare's, and the pair regularly socialised together. Kelly, who had groomed many of the city's most notorious criminals, was described by O'Hare as part of the *'terrible beauty'* of the Irish struggle against British colonialism, a direct reference to the great Irish poet W.B. Yeats. O'Hare also described Kelly as a *'martyr'* for Irish Republicanism. O'Hare went further and astonishingly compared his late friend to Jesus.

O'Hare said, "On a more spiritual note, I would like to emphasise the sacredness of Eamon's life as a reflection of Christ's life. Eamon, as you know, had suffered. Jesus, too, was sent by the Father to suffer."

O'Hare was applauded as he left the altar. All I can say to this is *God help us all!*

Dissident republican Sean Connolly pleaded guilty to Eamon Kelly's murder in 2015 and was sentenced to life imprisonment. Recently, another man, Darren Murphy, was convicted of the murder of Eamon Kelly by the Special Criminal Court and sentenced to life imprisonment. Murphy had carried out surveillance on Eamon Kelly two days before his murder and also on the day of the murder. Murphy was convicted on 15th November 2021.

In 1993, George Allis moved his business from North Circular Road to Parnell Street. It was here that I got a call from a financial journalist, the late Des Crowley. He was working for the now-defunct *Irish Press*. Mr Crowley was preparing an article on the progress of the Carpetdrome liquidation for the financial pages of the *Irish Press*. As the last court case was nine years earlier, I was out of touch with what was going on and was not of much help to him. This was the only time in forty years that I was approached by a journalist in connection with the affairs of Carpetdrome, despite the case being a very high-profile one.

In June 1996, I left George Allis' employment as he was finishing up his furnishing business to concentrate on his property business. Courts Furnishers were recruiting for their flagship store on the Naas Road and offered me a position. I spent a month training in the store before it opened. There was considerable unease amongst some staff about working with me as I was a former protected state witness. The British management became aware of this. They backed me because what I did was what they would expect of their employees. The Irish took a different view and were not keen on people who gave evidence for the state. The court cases back in the 1980s were still fresh in some people's minds.

On 26th June 1996, I was working in the Courts Store on the Naas Road. This was the day that Veronica Guerin was shot dead at Newlands Cross, about one mile away from the store. In June 1999, Brian Meehan was tried for his role in the murder of Veronica Guerin. My old classmate, Peter Charleton, prosecuted for the State. When opening the case, Mr Peter Charleton SC told the Special Criminal Court that the case was unique because it was the first time the Irish State had used a witness protection programme. Fancy that! I was the first person in the history of the State to enter a witness protection programme back in 1983.

Peter Charleton and I were in the same class in school in St Mary's College, Rathmines, for eleven years. Between 1972 and 1974, we studied together for the Leaving Certificate during the lunch break between 12.30 pm and 2.00 pm. I never went home for lunch because I lived on the north side of the city. Peter Charleton never went home for lunch either. The rest of the pupils went home for lunch, leaving the two of us in the classroom where we prepared for the Leaving Certificate together over the two years. It was an extraordinary coincidence that, in later years, Peter Charleton would become the leading prosecutor for the State, and I would become the first person in the history of the Irish State to enter a witness protection programme. You couldn't make it up. As well as that, both of us were on the school debating team. Both our fathers were well acquainted with each other through the drapery trade, and they were both members of the Castle Golf Club.

When Peter Charleton introduced the state witnesses, in the Veronica Guerin murder trial, to the Special Criminal Court as the first participants in a witness protection programme, he, above all people, knew the correct identity of the first participant. The murder of Veronica Guerin did not initiate the State's first witness protection programme; rather, it was my defection to the liquidator in the Kelly Case in 1983 that initiated it. As a result of this, Brian Meehan did not get a fair trial.

Peter Charleton is the co-author with Paul McDermott of the leading textbook on criminal law in Ireland called *Criminal Law and Evidence*. He is also the author of another legal textbook called *Criminal Law Cases and Materials* and has also published numerous texts on criminal law for various journals. Charleton is also an adjunct professor of criminal law and criminology at Galway University. He was the leading prosecutor for the State in the Guerin murder trials. All of this made him the leading authority on criminal law in Ireland. So, how could he not get a simple thing like the State's first witness protection programme, right? At home, my mother and I were astounded by Peter Charleton's claim that the witnesses in the Veronica Guerin murder trials were participants in the State's first-ever witness programme. Such was my anger with Peter Charleton that I avoided class reunions. If I had attended a class reunion, I would have given him an earful. John Gilligan, the leader of the gang that murdered Veronica Guerin, was later acquitted of her murder in the Special Criminal Court. As far as I am concerned, John Gilligan was connected with one murder, while Eamon Kelly was connected with seven murders. In my opinion, John Gilligan was only an apprentice compared to Eamon Kelly. Peter Charleton is now a judge of the Supreme Court.

The director of public prosecutions, who directed the prosecution of Brian Meehan for the murder of Veronica Guerin, was Eamonn Barnes. He was Ireland's first director of public prosecutions, and he retired in September 1999. He was the director of public prosecutions throughout my witness protection programme. It was Eamonn Barnes who made the decision not to prosecute the Kelly brothers. It was the same DPP who had my statement on his desk, alleging corruption against Haughey, and did absolutely nothing about it. Mr Barnes passed away on 1st November 2017.

The Minister for Justice Charles Flanagan led the tributes with the following statement: "Mr Barnes has served the State with considerable distinction in that role for 25 years, establishing the unquestioned independence from government."

Well, Mr Flanagan, I am now about to question that independence. The failure of Mr Barnes to acknowledge the State's first witness protection programme because it linked Haughey to organised crime clearly demonstrates that the office of the Director of Public Prosecutions is under political control and that the office is not the independent office that it would like to portray to the public. By concealing the State's first witness protection programme, the office of the Director of Public Prosecutions is participating in a political cover-up. The DPP's refusal to acknowledge the State's first witness protection programme shows contempt for the judiciary of this country because there was a judicial input into the initiation of the State's first witness protection programme. Mr Justice Costello had held that the business of Carpetdrome was carried on with intent to defraud creditors and for other fraudulent purposes, and he referred the case to the DPP at the end of a two-week trial.

Haughey's personal wealth and extravagant lifestyle were a source of curiosity to the general Irish public, who were aware that Haughey lived in a Gandon-designed mansion, had an island off the south west coast of Ireland called Inishvickillane, had a sailing yacht called Celtic Mist, and also owned several racehorses, all of this financed by a government salary. Following a dispute between Ben Dunne and his siblings, the government set up a tribunal led by Judge Brian McCracken in 1997. The purpose of the tribunal was to investigate secret payments from Ben Dunne Jnr to Charles Haughey, Michael Lowry, and others. As mentioned earlier, Brian McCracken SC represented Gaynor & Tuffy in the 1984 proceedings taken by Patrick Byrne, the liquidator of Carpetdrome.

Haughey gave evidence before the tribunal on 15th July 1997. The tribunal reported on 25th August 1997. The tribunal revealed that Haughey had received substantial monetary gifts from businessmen and that he had held secret offshore bank accounts in the Ansbacher Bank in the Cayman Islands. The McCracken Tribunal considered Mr Haughey's evidence to be unacceptable and untrue. McCracken cited 11 different incidences in which he described the former Taoiseach's evidence as *'not believable,' 'quite unbelievable,' 'most unlikely,' 'beyond all credibility'* or *'incomprehensible.'*

Also in 1997, the public was shocked by allegations that Haughey had embezzled money destined for the Fianna Fáil party. This was taxpayers' money taken from government funds earmarked for the operation of a political party, and Haughey spent a large portion of these funds on Charvet shirts and expensive dinners in a top Dublin restaurant, while preaching belt-tightening and implementing budget cuts as a national policy.

The Moriarty Tribunal was set up by the government in 1997 to investigate payments to politicians following the McCracken Tribunal report. The Moriarty Tribunal delved further into Haughey's financial affairs. The main report of the Moriarty Tribunal, which dealt with Charles Haughey, was released on 19th December 2006, about six months after his death. Mr Justice Moriarty found that Haughey was paid more than IR£8 million between 1979 and 1986 from various benefactors and businessmen, including IR£1.3 million from Ben Dunne Jnr. Moriarty found that IR£270,000 was raised in donations for a liver transplant for Brian Lenihan, but only IR£70,000 was spent on Lenihan's medical care. The tribunal found evidence of favours performed in return for money. Saudi businessman, Mahmoud Fustok, paid Haughey IR£50,000 to support applications for Irish passports. The tribunal found other evidence of favours performed. Haughey had arranged meetings between Ben Dunne Jnr and Seamus Pairceir, chairman of the Revenue Commissioners. These meetings resulted in an outstanding Capital Gains Tax Liability for Ben Dunne Jnr being significantly reduced. Moriarty found that this was *'not coincidental'* and that it was a substantial benefit conferred on Ben Dunne Jnr by Haughey. Moriarty also found that AIB settled Haughey's IR£1 million overdraft shortly after he became Taoiseach in 1979 and that this leniency amounted to an indirect payment by the bank to Haughey. Moriarty rejected Haughey's claims of ignorance of his own financial affairs, and Haughey was accused by the tribunal of *'devaluing democracy.'*

Despite having named Haughey as the recipient of a payment from Matt Kelly in the longest statement ever taken by the guards following an investigation ordered by a High Court judge, I was not summoned by the tribunal to give evidence. If I had been summoned, then I would have appeared at the tribunal and told the truth. I decided not to come forward to the tribunal because I was living at home with my mother. I felt that my mother had suffered enough back in the 1980s, as we had two uniformed Garda at the house around the clock, as well as my own personal protection. Her health was deteriorating, and I was concerned about the effect of the publicity on her that an appearance at the tribunal would generate. In October 2004, I arrived home from work late one evening and found her unresponsive on the kitchen floor.

I feel that my allegations about a payment by Matt Kelly to Charles Haughey, in May 1981, whereby a favour was sought by Kelly from Haughey, were prima facie evidence of a bribe. These allegations were made by me in September 1983 in two paragraphs in the longest statement ever taken by the guards in a criminal investigation ordered by a former attorney general and High Court judge, Mr Justice Declan Costello. The response of the guards was to try to pressurise me into withdrawing these two paragraphs, which I refused to do. The guards and the Irish State did nothing else about these allegations other than initiate a cover-up. If the State had done something back in 1983 about Haughey, the taxpayer could have been saved up to IR£90 million, as the two tribunals would never have been set up.

Another tribunal of inquiry that I could have made an impact on was the Smithwick Tribunal. The Smithwick's Tribunal was a tribunal of inquiry into the events surrounding the killing of Chief Superintendent Harry Breen and Superintendent Robert Buchanan of the Royal Ulster Constabulary. The men were killed in a Provisional IRA ambush near the Irish border at Jonesborough on 20th March 1989 as they returned in an unmarked car from a cross-border security conference in Dundalk with senior Garda officers. The tribunal issued its report on 3rd December 2013. In the report, Judge Smithwick said that he was satisfied that there was collusion in the murders. He also said that he was satisfied that the evidence points to the fact that there was someone within Dundalk Garda station assisting the IRA. If the judge had heard evidence from me about the existence of a Provisional IRA mole operating at the heart of the Special Detective Unit in Harcourt Square, Dublin, I doubt that he could have come to the conclusion that there was collusion between guards in Dundalk Garda station and the Provisional IRA in relation to the killings.

Thomas Oliver was a 43-year-old farmer from County Louth. He was tortured and murdered by the Provisional IRA in July 1991. Oliver had discovered a cache of arms hidden on his farm on the Cooley peninsula, which belonged to the Provisional IRA. He reported his findings to the local Garda. I have no doubt that the local Garda reported the discovery of arms to the Special Detective Unit in Harcourt Square and that this came to the attention of the Provisional IRA mole, who then fed this information back to the Provisional IRA. I have no doubt that the murders of Judge Gibson and his wife, RUC officers Harry Breen and Robert Buchanan, and farmer Thomas Oliver were linked to the Provisional IRA mole in Harcourt Square. I say this in the context of the two warnings that I got from Chief Superintendent Ned Ryan about the existence of the Provisional IRA mole back in 1983.

In January 1984, Matthew Kelly was declared bankrupt. In June 1987, the liquidator, Patrick Byrne, applied for court orders on the basis that the winding up of the company had been completed, and Byrne was discharged as liquidator. The official assignee in bankruptcy fixed 31st July 1997 as the last day on which creditors' proof of debt was to be received by him in the bankruptcy of Matthew Kelly. No proof of IR£1.9m debt was filed by that date.

In May 2001, the reappointed liquidator, Mr Tom Grace, applied to the High Court for more time to prove the debt against Matthew Kelly. Refusing the application, Mr Justice McCracken said that the 13-year delay in making the application prejudiced Matthew Kelly in that it would mean that he would have to find a further sum of €900,000 to become discharged from bankruptcy. By not proving the Carpetdrome debt before being discharged as a liquidator in 1987, the liquidator had abandoned his claim.

I find it extraordinary that Mr Justice Brian McCracken should be presiding over this case in 2002 because he represented Gaynor & Tuffy accountants in the 1984 hearing taken by the liquidator. The application was made following an investigation into the affairs of Matthew Kelly by the Criminal Assets Bureau, which uncovered substantial assets.

The murders of journalist Veronica Guerin and Detective Garda Jerry McCabe in 1996 paved the way for the Criminal Assets Bureau. The CAB was set up by the Oireachtas in October 1996 as a body corporate primarily for the purpose of ensuring that persons should not benefit from any assets acquired by them from any criminal activity. It was given powers to take all necessary actions in relation to seizing and securing assets derived from criminal activity, certain powers to ensure that the proceeds of such activity are subject to tax, and also in relation to the *Social Welfare Acts*. However, as the High Court has noted, it is not a prosecuting body nor a police authority but rather it is an investigating authority which, having investigated and used its powers of investigation, then applies to the High Court for assistance in enforcing its functions.

One of the first targets of the CAB was Matt Kelly. They used their newly acquired powers to investigate his affairs. Although having been declared a bankrupt in 1984 on the application of the Carpetdrome liquidator, CAB documents showed that he was the beneficial owner of an extensive property portfolio. He denied that his properties were funded from the proceeds of crime. He protested that his properties were funded from borrowings. The CAB documents claimed that Matt Kelly was the beneficial owner of 15 commercial properties worth IR€10 million. These included numbers 345, 346, 347, 349 North Circular Road, numbers 38, 39, 40, 41, 42, 43, 44, 45 Talbot Street, and numbers 14, 15, 16 Foley Street. The CAB documents also claimed that he controlled three nursing homes in Lincolnshire through a company called *Argento Properties*. CAB handed Kelly a tax assessment for €3 million. The bill was increased to IR£3.6m due to interest added on as Kelly delayed in settling. This bill forced Kelly to sell some of his properties, and, thus, he generated further capital gains tax liabilities. He then paid IR£4m to the CAB in settlement of his income tax and capital gains tax liabilities and was released from bankruptcy. He wasn't left penniless either, as the properties he retained were very valuable.

The Kelly carpet cases were the first major confrontation between the Irish State and organised crime. With the benefit of hindsight, I don't think that the State wanted any criminal prosecutions; the State just wanted its taxes. The conviction for criminal contempt of court against Matt Kelly and Michael Deighan was quashed. Neither Matt Kelly nor his brother Eamon Kelly was prosecuted for the Carpetdrome's fraudulent trading. Nor were they prosecuted for the fire that destroyed the carpet retail premises. Michael Deighan also escaped prosecution for perjury.

Paddy Byrne, the liquidator, was discharged from his duties in 1987 by the High Court. He continued working in Coopers & Lybrand until his retirement in 1995, when he turned 70. One summer's evening in 1995, George Allis and I went to measure a house for curtains in Donnybrook. Afterwards, we paid a visit to Madigan's bar on Morehampton Road. In the bar, a well-attended party was in full flow. It was Paddy Byrne's retirement party. When Byrne spotted me, he came over and asked me what I was doing there. He appeared to be shocked at my presence as if a ghost had come back to haunt him. To calm him down, I explained that George and I were just passing and decided to drop in for a drink. The last person he expected or wanted to see near his retirement party was me. Paddy Byrne passed away on Tuesday, 19th October 2021, at the age of 96. At the time of his death, he was the oldest former TD, the longest surviving Dáil member, and the only surviving member of the 15th Dáil.

Mr Richard Cooke SC continued practising law until he was in his 90s. As such, he was the oldest working barrister, which earned him the title *'Father of the Bar.'* He passed away on 1st January 2007, aged 94.

His son, Mr John Cooke SC, was appointed by the Irish government to the Court of First Instance of the European Communities in January 1996. He retired from this court in September 2008. He was then appointed a judge of the High Court in November 2008. He retired from this position in December 2013. In 2014, he headed an inquiry into the alleged bugging of the Garda Siochana Ombudsman Commission (GSOC), and he found no evidence of surveillance by the force. He also served as president of the Zoological Society of Ireland from 1987 to 1989. I could not think of a better place for him than up in the zoo with the monkeys! He passed away on 28th April 2022.

Mr Peter Kelly SC was appointed a High Court judge in 1996. He was then appointed presiding judge of the Commercial Court in 2004. The Commercial Court is a division within the High Court. He was then appointed to the Court of Appeal in 2014. He was made president of the High Court in 2015, a position from which he retired in 2020.

Mr Thomas Tuite, who headed the revenue investigation into the affairs of Carpetdrome and Matt Kelly, was based in the Special Investigations Branch in Setanta House in Nassau Street. In 1986, he was moved from here to the VAT office in Sandymount.

Eileen Hogg, whose position in the Carpetdrome I filled in 1979, following her departure to Canada, gave birth to a baby boy called Aidan in June 1983. Aidan Turner is the actor who plays the role of *Ross Poldark* in the popular BBC TV series, *Poldark*. Another person, connected with the Carpetdrome, who has made a career in acting, is Derek Reddin. Derek plays the role of *Dr Flynn* in Brendan O'Carroll's sitcom, *Mrs*

Brown's Boys. I mentioned Derek earlier in the book as the recipient of some nasty treatment from Eamon Kelly.

As for myself, I ended up long-term unemployed, having been made redundant in 2010. The redundancy was caused by the banking crisis. I was out of work for five years, and I only got back to work through a state-subsidised two-year job placement programme. If you have got this far, thank you for persevering with me.

www.ingramcontent.com/pod-product-compliance
Lightning Source LLC
Chambersburg PA
CBHW052058070526
44584CB00017B/2230